BARRENNESS AND BLESSING

BARRENNESS AND BLESSING

ABRAHAM, SARAH, AND THE JOURNEY OF FAITH

HEMCHAND GOSSAI

CASCADE *Books* • Eugene, Oregon

BARRENNESS AND BLESSING
Abraham, Sarah, and the Journey of Faith

Cascade Books
A Division of Wipf and Stock Publishers
199 W. 8th Ave., Suite 3
Eugene, OR 97401

ISBN 13: 978-1-55635-292-8

Cataloging-in-Publication data:

Gossai, Hemchand.
    Barrenness and blessing : Abraham, Sarah, and the journey of faith /
    Hemchand Gossai.

    xiv + 122 p.; 22 cm.
    Includes bibliographical references (p. 121–122).

    ISBN 13: 978-1-55635-292-8

    1. Bible. O.T. Genesis—Criticism, interpretation, etc. 2. Abraham (Biblical
Patriarch). 3. Sarah (Biblical Matriarch). 4. Jacob (Biblical Patriarch). I. Title.

BS580 .A3 G67 2008

Manufactured in the U.S.A.

Blessed for the Journey

For Nathan, Krista, Chandra, and Zachary

CONTENTS

PREFACE

THE ABRAHAM NARRATIVES have occupied my attention for a number of years, and I am struck by their persistent relevance not only for intellectual pondering and inquiry but also for their pointed connection with our contemporary world. The exploration in these narratives of themes such as wilderness and freedom, barrenness and hope, wrestling and blessing strike a chord with many of us—a chord that refuses to be silenced.

Thanks to K. C. Hanson for his interest in this project and his invitation to publish it, and for the staff at Wipf and Stock whose remarkable care gave this book an unmistakable quality.

INTRODUCTION

IN BOTH THE Hebrew Bible and the New Testament, particular themes, or even verses, emerge as foundational or central. Indeed some parts have been elevated to such places of prominence that they have gained universal acclaim. In this regard, certainly Psalm 23 and John 3:16 come readily to mind. And while it is the case that there is some value here, it strikes me that we ought not isolate sections of the text at the expense of the whole. In the case of the Abraham narratives, perhaps not surprisingly, the faith of Abraham, his righteousness, and God's promises to him and Sarah are given prominence. One could understand this emphasis, as the focus of these themes is positive, is not overly challenging, and (most important) is central to Christian belief. However, the entirety of these narratives is lengthy and complex; to reduce the difficult and complex parts to the most understandable and satisfying common denominator is to do a disservice to the text.

As I read the Abraham narratives, I am immediately struck by the human drama and the divine involvement in all aspects of the human journey. This drama, it seems to me, is exactly the broad point of departure for entering the story in a way that allows the story the possibility of becoming our story. Thus we discern in the story both the strengths and frailties of what it means to be human: the possibilities and the shortcomings, the persistence of faith together with moments of challenging doubts. Equally or perhaps more important, the narrative tells us something about God, about the nature of God and the manner in which God functions in the world. Thus, as surprising as it is to begin a new journey with barrenness, this surprising beginning, in fact, tells us more about God than about Sarah and Abraham. What shapes the journey of creation is not only what God is able to do but, in fact, how and where God will choose to begin this story. Thus, barrenness is also our invitation to imagine as the divine is able to imagine; and perhaps not surprisingly, while Abraham and Sarah believed and trusted God, it is equally clear that like all humans, they faltered, but were not abandoned.

The nature of our society has perhaps caused certain themes of the Abraham stories to recede into the shadows. Neither barrenness nor wilderness holds any great existential fear today. To be sure, the issue of fertility remains a factor—though it can be and is attended to in a variety of ways. But while the literal qualities of these themes are no longer pointedly relevant, in my view they have taken on a pronounced metaphorical importance.

The Abraham narratives form a significant component of the ancestral narratives in the book of Genesis. The opening line of the story of Abraham and Sarah announces an extraordinary reality. As readers, we realize that peoples and nations will be born out of this couple; that Sarah's barrenness becomes the principal focus of the story is particularly striking. From the beginning we know that "barrenness" will halt the future prospects for Abraham and Sarah, and it is beyond their control to transform this reality. Yet, it is precisely in the state of barrenness that promises of blessing and fulfillment come. From the outset, it is also clearly established that God will proceed from a point of challenge, as humans conceive of challenge. God proceeds outside of convention and norm. The barren receive a promise; hope comes to those who live beyond conventional hope; fulfillment comes despite constricted norms.

In this study it is precisely the tension between challenge and hope that is explored. The Abraham narratives provide for us an invitation to enter into the stories and in important ways, to allow them to become our stories. The themes of the stories are profoundly human themes. They capture the persistent interaction between God and humankind. As human beings, we are invited to witness the manner in which God enters human community in all its complexities, struggles, challenges, fears, and, ultimately, in its hope. As the Abraham story unfolds, not only is it clear that God will not be restricted by societal and cultural convention, but that the human journey will be generated by faith and doubt, fear and hope, promise and fulfillment, all the while shaped by God, the architect and navigator.

In this study I will not only explore the various themes within a variety of passages, but also I will maintain a constant eye on the implications for contemporary readers. In this regard, some of the literal and particular experiences such as *barrenness, wilderness, and wrestling with God* will be examined as metaphors for our experiences. The richness and texture of these metaphors allow us to enter these stories in a way that makes them our stories.

1

THE CHALLENGE
OF BARRENNESS

BARRENNESS IS LIKELY to tell us more about the way God proceeds than about the human who feels trapped in various states of barrenness. If indeed barrenness represents the end of a future or a death of sorts, God, as we see in these narratives, is unafraid to begin from this point. Barrenness is established as a possible place for yet another starting point for newness. Barreness also poses for the human being a challenge to believe beyond what is immediately apparent—certainly a challenge not to be taken lightly.

When taken either literally or figuratively, the idea of barrenness bodes ill for the future. Whether it is the barrenness of a land that is parched and dry with no prospects for life, or the barrenness of Sarah and Abraham who, now in their elderly years, have resigned themselves to not having offspring. Barrenness ultimately leads to resignation and to the belief that the present reality is the way things will always be, and there is no vision for the unfolding of a future beyond one's capacity to see. Thus, hope dies in the face of barrenness. The challenge of barrenness then is not only to accept a particular reality of the present, but also to imagine that it is not the last word, that the final divine word is yet to be spoken and eventuated.

The fact that the Abraham narrative begins with an iteration of Sarah's barrenness establishes that this will be a persistent challenge to the future of Abraham and Sarah. That the challenge of barrenness comes on the heels of the genealogy of Terah, Abraham's father (Gen 11:10–29), makes clear that if barrenness continues for Abraham and Sarah, then their story and lineage will indeed come to an end. Yet, ironically, as if to set the challenge of the promise of descendants in sharp relief against the genealogy, the narrator begins the story of Abraham and Sarah with barrenness. Yet, how can barrenness become a door to new life and not, as it is conventionally understood, the final word? This is the challenge.

The reality of Sarah's barrenness is juxtaposed against the tripartite promise that God makes to Abraham for 1) land, 2) descendants, and 3) blessing (Gen 12:1–3). Notable here is that promises in the face of barrenness are made without a timeline, the very thing most of us would naturally seek. Instead a new future is spoken of, and neither God nor Abraham broaches the "when" question. The language of the text is spare and terse, but the underlying issue is unmistakable. How might these promises be embraced and believed in the face of barrenness? The very pronouncement of the promises establishes a change in Abraham and Sarah's reality, for these divine words carry the power and force of fulfillment. Can Abraham and Sarah's faith have a future? Do they have the requisite faith beyond their human vision?

Sarah's barrenness, however, is but a beginning. To the degree that barrenness might be construed as that which places a "period" after the "sentence" of the present, then Abraham and Sarah's immediate journey to the land of Canaan, and their discovering a populated land poses another expression of barrenness, in the sense that on the surface, it appears that there is no way toward the promise of attaining the land (Gen 12:6). Without any elaboration, Abraham and Sarah are simply told that the land of Canaan will be theirs, and again in that moment Abraham believes (v. 7). Belief of such extraordinary magnitude under ordinary circumstances is remarkable, but in the face of barrenness, such belief is truly remarkable. The transformation from the present reality of security and settledness had begun, but not without significant hurdles. Whatever glimpses Sarah and Abraham have of the future seem to be blocked. Not only does Sarah and Abraham's old age defy childbearing, but also old age coupled with Sarah's lifelong barrenness seem to eliminate any prospect of having children. Further, the irony of the "fullness" of the land poses a particular kind

of barrenness, for both descendants and land are prerequisites for nationhood, and the land of promise is already populated. Under these
circumstances, the prospects of Abraham being a blessing to others
seems to be a particular challenge.

Yet, in view of these many expressions of barrenness, Abraham
and Sarah nevertheless begin their journey without objection, without
question—a posture remarkable under any circumstances. It is evident
from the beginning that this journey will pose for them unique challenges. They cannot of their accord undo the state of barrenness or
empty an occupied land. Thus, their journey begins and must proceed
on faith. This is a journey that will generate many questions and challenges by Abraham and Sarah, most of which are directed at God. But
at the outset, it is God who announces, and humans respond. God,
as architect of the promise and journey, is recognized as such when
Abraham builds an altar to God and worships (Gen 12:7).

THEMES OF BARRENNESS IN GENESIS AND IN
CONTEMPORARY LIFE

Genesis 11:30 begins with the dramatic pronouncement that Sarah is
barren. As in any great narrative beginning, this beginning marks a
governing theme in the story. Yet even as the theme of barrenness is
mentioned prominently, the narrative seemingly continues in a different direction. Still, it is clear that Sarah's barrenness is not a detail to
be dismissed. The wider narrative of Genesis, which to this point has
recounted various genealogies, seems to bring to an end any future
prospects for this particular family. Genesis 11 ends with a note of
present death (Terah's demise) and with the death of a future (Sarah's
barrenness). Whatever else will transpire in this narrative, certainly
Abraham and Sarah's journey will not be ordinary, and in no way will
it be easy or straightforward. Moreover, by beginning with barrenness, this narrative sensitizes its audience to a new reality: this state
of barrenness will not always be the way it is. The double statement in
11:30 ("Now Sarai was barren; she had no child") emphasizes Sarah's
barrenness, but then this detail remains unattended, as if the narrator
intends to plant this seed of barrenness in the minds of the readers,
with the hint of what is to come. As one generation comes to an end

with the death of Terah, the prospects for Abraham's generation to end without posterity loom large, and one is sharply reminded that Sarah is barren; Sarah and Abraham do not have a child. The present is clear, and unless something extraordinary happens, the future is also set to end. In the face of such barrenness, then, what might one hope for? The challenge of barrenness takes one beyond the present, to imagine a future that seems impossible in the light of the present circumstances. Certainly the particularity of Sarah's barrenness is very clear; on a personal level, she will not be able to experience the quintessential expression of motherhood—that defining quality of womanhood in ancient Israel. Yet, as important as this deprivation is, barrenness (as we witness it in this narrative) ushers in a broader and more complex picture for humanity. I suggest that barrenness in the context of this narrative has universal implications. A sharp juxtaposition occurs between, on the one hand, the theme or tone of death at the end of Genesis 11, and, on the other hand, the unexplained, equally surprising pronouncement of newness, and the break from the past as Genesis 12 begins. Newness will happen in the context of barrenness, and this means that human beings' faith and trust not only will be essential but also will be put to the test.

Even beyond the particularity of Sarah's barrenness, the promise of land to Abraham and his ancestors is dramatic; the promise of a land brings a more definitive sense of belonging. Indeed the physical barrenness of Sarah clearly relates to the barrenness of landlessness. With the promise of the land comes the distinct possibility of a new sense of belonging. Both the promise of progeny and the promise of land will take enormous faith, as neither seems possible as far as Abraham and Sarah's horizon extends. Abraham and Sarah's faithful step in departing Haran indicates willingness and trust; but, as we shall see from the narrative, what will be essential is *sustained trust*. As if these challenges were not enough, the reality is that both Abraham and Sarah are old. Thus, journeying to land and offspring (both beyond their capacity) will test their trust to the very limit.

Whereas Genesis 1 begins with what some scholars refer to as *creatio ex nihilo* or *order out of chaos*, Genesis 12 begins differently; it begins with promise of a future. However, it is the verses that connect the primeval history of Genesis 1–11 to the ancestral narratives of

Genesis 12–20 that in fact strike a marked chord of resonance. If, in fact, it would take divine initiative to bring creation out of nothing or order out of chaos, then it would involve equally divine initiative to bring about a people out of barrenness. Such is the dramatic reminder in Genesis 11:30, that indeed it would take nothing less than a divine working. In both Genesis 1 and Genesis 12, God's presence and active generating are essential. In the case of human understanding, beginning from a state of nothingness is out of the realm of reality. However, in Genesis 1 and 12, God employs barrenness, both literally and metaphorically, as a point of beginning. Without ever stating the obvious, the text establishes that God is able to bring creation into being from any source—including from a source unimaginable to human beings. Moreover, given human finitude, it will take more than humankind's capacity for reason or knowledge to enter into such a realm of creation.

That is to say, humans will have to envision, imagine, believe, and trust. Indeed barrenness invokes precisely these qualities in humankind, for barrenness is to be seen as a divine *comma* as opposed to a human *period*. Indeed the very drama of the Abraham narrative depends overwhelmingly on the role of barrenness. Within human history, it would certainly be conventional to begin something new from a point of strength. By design, God's hope and plan for a future is planted firmly in a barren context. From a human perspective, this might appear to undermine the establishment of a future. Yet, from the outset, the text has established the nature of hope. Hope receives its finest and sharpest definition in the context of what appears to be hopeless and barren. Indeed hope only has a fullness of meaning when generated from a state of hopelessness. We not only discover that Sarah is barren, but also that the land is inhabited; thus at the very outset, the stark and complex reality is that both emptiness and fullness are expressions of barrenness. Why would God choose to begin at such devastating points? Placement, displacement, and replacement all converge. It is not within the power of Abraham and Sarah to have a child together as it stands, anymore than it is possible for Abraham and Sarah to empty the land of Canaan. While it is the case that "this God does not depend on any potentiality in the one addressed,"[1] and thus God establishes God's self very clearly as the architect of this newness, nonetheless humans play an essential role in its fulfillment. Even as the "spoken word" in Genesis 1 generated a defined universe, also the spoken word to Abraham in the face of barrenness will generate newness. The power of the divinely spoken word is evidenced throughout Scripture: from Moses to Elijah, from Eli to Jeremiah. What we are assured of is that nothing is beyond the scope of God, and that God will use whomever God chooses—even the old and barren and those who cannot envision beyond the present. This is a manner of suggesting that human barrenness in all of its manifestations is tied to faith.

In the crucifixion and resurrection accounts in the Gospels, it was widely believed by those closest to Jesus that the crucifixion is an end. The idea that life might emerge from death seems inconceivable despite the many representations of such emerging life throughout the ministry of Jesus. Throughout the Hebrew Bible and the New Testament, it remains the case that God intentionally begins from a "barren" state. From the physical barrenness of Sarah, Rebekah, Rachel, and Hannah; from David, ill-qualified to be king, to Peter, the Rock; from Rahab to Mary Magdalene. Barrenness, in fact, is the norm for God and thus stands in marked contrast to human conventions for the launching of newness.

Yet, as if Sarah's barrenness were not enough, the theme of dislocation is introduced. Abraham, Sarah, and others are asked to leave their sense of security, and journey into the unknown. In order for Abraham and his descendants to find a place—a land—it would first mean a sense of displacement, for them to take the extraordinary risk to dislocate, and with no particular idea of what to expect (Gen 12:3–4).

As the narrative begins, two themes become inseparable, namely, heirship and family. Both of these are placed within the context of barrenness. Thus from the beginning, by human standards the progression of the future appears dark and close to ending. The mention of Lot in Genesis 11:27, and the clearly identified barrenness of Sarah ("Now Sarai was barren; she had no child" [11:30]) accentuate the suspense of the future. No explicit indication is given for Lot's accompanying Abraham except perhaps for the juxtaposition of Lot with

---

1. Brueggemann, *Genesis*, 117.

the barrenness of Sarai, and the early textual allusion that Lot would become the heir of Abraham—a customary solution to the heirship dilemma. This mention of Lot as Abraham's heir is a striking allusive note as to the textual plans for the future. Even as the narrative proceeds, it becomes apparent that conventional human constructs, important as they are, will not suffice. Perhaps the lack of specificity in Genesis 12:1–3 about the way that the promised heir will be fulfilled might very well lead readers to conclude that Lot might be the presumptive heir; or readers might be persuaded, more notably, by Genesis 15, where Abraham wonders to God whether Eliezer of Damascus will be his heir (v. 2). Again the divine assurance is given without specifics. With this ongoing pattern, the Abraham narratives are held in a constant state of suspense.

With the call out of barrenness for Abraham and Sarah, we witness a gradual movement to the center of existence. This movement from marginality to centrality is seen in at least two ways. Clearly barrenness as a state of marginality is evident throughout the Abraham narratives. But as Fretheim has noted, "the family . . . enables God's cosmic purposes and activity."[2] God makes a clear case for the role of the particular in shaping the universal. The family unit, so emphasized in the opening section of the Abraham narratives, will not be an end in itself. The family unit, immediate and extended (including women, albeit sparsely), becomes the centerpiece. Barrenness has a veiled manner of protecting itself and providing its own identity by separation. We have such an evident moment in Genesis 11, when the people seek a distinct unity born out of separation (v. 4), but, in fact, God chooses scattering. By human conventions, togetherness can never be defined by scattering. Such is the nature of how God typically begins. The family is called from "*your country, your kindred, your father's house to the land*" (Gen 12:1). This is the land for all, not only for one. That is, barrenness becomes a point of departure for a movement and understanding of one family to the families of the earth. The very geography and trajectory of Abraham and Sarah's journey suggest a marked shift in direction. God begins from the margins and journeys to the center, a striking reorientation of societal conventions.

2. Fretheim, "Genesis," 425.

If, as it appears, the rhythm of Abraham and Sarah's life is a relentless movement to an inevitable end, then God disrupts the rhythm of their lives with a startling reversal that goes beyond anything they can imagine: bearing the promise of progeny and all that this entails. Equally remarkable is the fact that their particularity will lead to a new kind of universality. If, then, particularity is as much of a challenge as it is, how can Abraham and Sarah begin to understand the universal implications?

In the beginning, from the perspective of barrenness, it appears that God takes an enormous risk. Perhaps one might even say that the magnitude of the risk reflects the scope of the promise for the future. In God's pronouncing promises from the state of Abraham and Sarah's barrenness, without any particular timeline, the narrative offers its inherent understanding that those who are called by God are in fact invited. The imperative "Follow me," to the disciples (Matt 5:19) is not a choiceless mandate but rather an invitation. Invitations, by definition, provide the option for and possibility of declining. As long as it is the case that God will work with and through human agency, the element of risk exists. Moreover, divine pronouncements bring with them the potential for misunderstanding and misinterpretation. As we witness today globally, the range of interpretation of the Bible among Christians might sometimes lead one to conclude that not everyone is reading the same text. Either by design or by accident, a text's voice might very well be drowned by our personal theological or ideological motivations. Thus when one is called and sent by God, hearing the message of promise must not be subsumed by human "voice."

The language of literal or figurative barrenness is the language of journeying. The call from barrenness is a call to travel into the unknown. In the New Testament, the call of the disciples is a call to travel into uncharted waters, and like Abraham, they will have to navigate murky waters, but there will not be negotiation with God. Barrenness for lengthy periods has the potential to cause us to imagine it in its varied form, as security; that is to say, as the known. Even though the known might move relentlessly to death, it is often weighed over against the unknown. If the unknown hints of fear, then security hints of barrenness. For one to leave a place of barrenness, one must consciously and intentionally loosen and disconnect the ties that bind, and begin a journey into the unknown. As Brueggemann concludes, "The whole of Abraham narrative is premised on this seeming contradiction: to stay in safety is to remain barren; to leave in risk is to have hope."[3] Certainly also there is a state of settledness in Haran, versus the unknown in Canaan. When the unknown in Canaan becomes known, the complexities only increase; for not only is the land occupied, but also Abraham's living within this occupied land is an early hint that his capacity for blessing will be put to the test (Gen 20). It is clear that in Genesis, barrenness is the avenue through which God generates families and generations. It runs contrary to human norms. This pattern continues with Isaac and Rebekah, where we become aware that Rebekah is barren. Unlike Abraham and Sarah, who hear the promises of God and express seemingly little immediate concern about Sarah's barrenness, both Isaac and Rebekah pray to God for different reasons, under different circumstances (Gen 25:21–22). In some measure, God answers both prayers—one in a conventional way, namely, that Rebekah conceives; God responds to the other prayer by overturning conventions, as we eavesdrop on the brief dialog between God and Rebekah in Genesis 25:22–23:

> The children struggled together within her; and she said, "If it is to be this way, why do I live?" So she went to inquire of the Lord. And the Lord said to her,
>
> "Two nations are in your womb, and two people born of you shall be divided; The one shall be stronger than the other, the elder shall serve the younger."

The juxtaposition of these two narratives (Abraham and Sarah, and Isaac and Rebekah) provides for us an entry into the complexity of both situations. We might wonder as to the reason for Abraham's silence regarding Sarah's barrenness, in the face of the promises. It would not be the only time that the silence of Abraham is conspicuous (see also Gen 22). While they might be understood and construed as trust, Isaac's, Rebekah's, and Hannah's prayers all point to the clear reality that God would and does act. It is the case, however, that Isaac and Rebekah believed that they might have a child. At the outset of his prayer (Gen 25:21), Isaac believes that Rebekah's barrenness is

3. Brueggemann, *Genesis*, 118.

not necessarily the end, and that barrenness need not be viewed as a future without prospect. It is, moreover, immediately understood that God was active, and finally the one responsible for life and for the movement from death to life. We are not privy to why, but without any further petitions or encumbrances, God hears and answers the prayer of Isaac. This particular moment certainly contrasts with the Abraham-and-Sarah episode, yet there is also a caution in the story of Isaac and Rebekah not to view too narrowly the prayer and response between Isaac and God. The prayer and response between Isaac and God appears to me to be a model for prayer. Yet, we must ask what manner of a model. Care must be taken not to take this particular moment out of context and apply it as a blanket statement of trust, as in fact some do. Is there faith, trust, belief here? Unequivocally yes! However, we must pursue a larger question: one that is not predicated on the idea that if one makes a request of God, then the request will be granted. Not only is this a misunderstanding and misrepresentation, but also this misunderstanding and misinterpretation leads more often to despair and heartache than to strength and trust.

By definition, journeys into the unknown take one over various kinds of terrain, and with the journey of Isaac, the future expands beyond the lives of Isaac and Rebekah, but the future also brings complexities beyond their imaginations. What we cannot overlook is the reality that conflict, division, and fear may all be a part of the fix. As much as the episode with Isaac and Rebekah points to a future, and to heirship for this couple, one must not overlook the reality of God as Creator in this episode. This theme is notably the recurring central theme throughout Genesis.

Clearly in the Abraham narratives, it is undoubtedly the case that God is the architect of the future. Particularly in the case of Isaac and Rebekah, it is certainly clear that God is the architect in matters pertaining to the future. But it is equally true that in shaping and defining the future, God does not proceed in conventionally human ways, and thus human control is deeply curtailed. In the case of Isaac and Rebekah, one might understand wilderness as expressed most notably in potential for conflict. Not only will there be conflict in the present, for there is a subtext of deceit between Rebekah and Isaac. Given God's plan to proceed with a future predicated on conflict, one must not be overly anxious to deride Rebekah in her actions. Literally and figuratively, Rebekah is also in a state of barrenness. She is aware that the divine decision to overturn the primogeniture convention will place her role as one of *persona non grata*. Barrenness for Rebekah comes also in the form of what might be construed as a secret divine promise (Gen 25:23). The promise, which pronounces a future, also keeps the present in a state of tension. Indeed one could argue that Rebekah sacrifices her future for the sake of the future of the promise. Rebekah's vulnerable state is pronounced.

The challenge of both ancestral families (Abraham and Sarah, Isaac and Rebekah) is that each movement out of barrenness—one not requested, the other sought—brings conflict and difficulties. In God's decision to bring about a future of new possibilities, human families will often find themselves in conflicted circumstances. Moreover, as we observed in the open-ended promises made to Abraham and Sarah, the reality is that the effects of barrenness will carry on from generation to generation; and as we shall discover, so does blessing. We are given a clear indication that God's creative actions set into motion a ripple effect that often merges with the lives of human existence; God will work through human realities.

There is yet a further issue at stake. In starting from a point of barrenness, God takes a risk. It is not the typical starting point for humans, and thus, as in matters of call, God clearly takes a chance of being misunderstood. How could it be expected that humans will see beyond the present? Yet, there is an expectation that in God's words to Rebekah, Rebekah receives a word about the future that she feels unable to share with others. We might further note that Rebekah, like Hannah, crosses boundaries and seeks out God personally and directly. In her interaction with God, Rebekah's personal interchange brings a word not to Isaac but to herself. In my view, Rebekah's silence and, ultimately, her decision to aid Jacob in deceiving Isaac (Gen 27:1–17) reflect the possibility that if this word were to escape, the community would not tolerate it. There are moments when barrenness is further compounded.

When Hagar conceives with Abraham (Gen 16:4), what Sarah sees might likely not have been what Hagar shows. Not only is the Hebrew ambiguous in this regard, but also the reality is that what we see and hear is also shaped by the circumstances in which we find ourselves. With Sarah's knowledge of Hagar's pregnancy, God's promise and gift of a future drift into the shadows of her consciousness. Depending on who has the knowledge, it is possible that there was some power, but knowledge does not come without some transformation in the community. For Sarah, the knowledge of Hagar's pregnancy with Abraham becomes a burden that would lead to a decision to exile her, by default. This is a stark reminder that Sarah's expectation and anticipation of the future would not be realized in quite the manner she expected.

In Genesis 3:4–6, Eve decides on the basis of her personal skill and theological assessment that it would be beneficial to eat of the fruit: on the surface, her logic appears sound and the reasoning well grounded. If, in fact, eating the fruit will bring knowledge, if it is good for sustenance and has aesthetic quality, then it seems virtually perfect. Yet, as the woman discovers, together with the hitherto silent man, this knowledge brings a new level of burden (v. 7). This knowledge certainly ushers in a startling awareness of being human. In many respects, at least in this case, being more fully human comes with a price. It would be difficult to argue that being more fully human is not a gift, in some regards; but this kind of knowledge also means that one is propelled to act differently. Certainly hindsight allows one to see the results of the new knowledge somewhat more sharply, and that perhaps is a luxury neither Eve nor Sarah nor Rebekah had. Knowledge brings with it a change of status, and invariably a variety of different conflicts.

In the case of Rebekah, her brief but pointed complaint to God ("If it is to be this way, why do I live?"[Gen 25:22]) sets into motion a series of events that she could never have anticipated. Arguably even more than Sarah's, Rebekah's knowledge will be something of a burden, for there is an inherent silence attached. Moreover, no evidence suggests that had Rebekah ventured to discuss with Isaac or with others her encounter with God that in fact she would have been believed. Rebekah in fact is never told not to discuss her divine encounter with anyone. We are never told why Rebekah makes a decision to keep silent, but she does, and her decision pointedly brings a redefinition of her life. Her decision is about neither weakness nor fear. In a state of barrenness when one has knowledge of the future that potentially overturns conventions, one has power. From her having known barrenness and the marginalization that comes therein, it is understandable that Rebekah would have seen her knowledge as a source of power.

Rebekah is in uncharted waters as she seeks to discern from God the discomfort of her pregnancy. There is no mediator here as Rebekah takes her torment directly to God, in itself a departure from convention. God's response to Rebekah unfolds a future plan, which clearly was not anticipated in her question. The knowledge that she carries has shed light on the internal conflict that she has experienced, but now the knowledge brings a grave external, fraternal, and national conflict. Internally, Rebekah must now struggle with whether she will tell Isaac of her "secret," or whether she will hold to the secret and allow the future to be shaped by God's plan and her actions. Clearly, loyalty has its place, and loyalty to Isaac might have a principal place, but this is to be held in tension with Rebekah's loyalty to herself. One, indeed, might argue that loyalty at all costs is no loyalty, and perhaps also in this case one could argue that honesty at all costs, without re-demptive value, is no virtue. In this case, however, honesty is not clear cut. Clearly not all knowledge will be freeing for Rebekah, and while in her pregnancy she is released from her state of barrenness, she now finds herself in another state of "private barrenness" as she holds within herself that which the world is unaware of, that which will re-cast the very future for which she longed. Both Sarah and Rebekah, in their natural waiting for motherhood and for the fulfillment of a divine promise, will also experience the pain and complexity of car-rying a promise. Despite the struggles of both Sarah and Rebekah, neither is disparaged or chastised by God.

It is difficult to find within the academy, and certainly within the church, those who sing the praises of Lot's daughters. These daughters find themselves in the middle of a complex, fearful, disturbing, and violent situation. They have little or no power and, not surprisingly, very little control of their destiny. Beyond the burning boundaries of Sodom and Gomorrah, they find themselves in a more precarious situation as they flee with their father, unable to take a final glance at either their home or their mother (Gen 19:16–17). Earlier, their father had abandoned them, offering them to the violent men of the city (Gen 19:4–8): men whose actions he had earlier deemed wicked

(v. 8). Then their mother had died (Gen 19:26). The daughters see and imagine their future as bleak; they see few prospects for children, and they see an imminent end to their lives. Regardless of what overstated myopia this might be, the daughters of Lot cannot see beyond the distant caves in which they found themselves. One might say that they not only see themselves desperate to experience motherhood; they see themselves as so desperate that they are willing to sacrifice their present reality for a future.

The general consensus among scholars and in the church is that the actions of the daughters are depraved, and yet I submit that this is *not* the whole story. Almost certainly there is an element of depravity. However, I submit additionally that the daughters face two prospects of barrenness, which in their eyes were of such extraordinary proportions that they could not possibly imagine viable options except for those that came readily to mind. First, while clearly they are not physically, literally barren, they face what they consider a *barren* future. As we have already discovered in the Abraham-and-Sarah narrative, the reality of barrenness and the prospects of no future invariably compel a person to act in a way that might seem contrary to both conscience and convention. The story of Lot's retreat into the cave could easily have ended without the additional nine verses in which the daughters intentionally seek to impregnate themselves through their father (Gen 19:30–38). Yet, here they are, and it seems that these verses serve a purpose greater than to create a scenario that allows for the condemnation of depravity or incest; but what is this greater purpose? Whether or not one can ever get close to certainty about the purpose of these verses, the reality is that this section of the narrative suggests that the daughters simply cast away their present for the possibility of a future. Taken by itself, sacrificing a present for a future at some level has some redemptive qualities to it. We see this kind of reckoning in Rebekah's action on behalf of Jacob in the deception of Isaac.

As this brief section of the Abraham narrative begins, it is apparent that Lot's life is shaped by two factors. First, he has evidently found a place of safety, far away in the hills (Gen 19:30). That seclusion becomes the manner of life is equally evident from Lot's earlier action involving his daughters (Gen 19:6–7). Their future, or for that matter the future of his "line," is not a factor for him. Second, Lot is motivated by fear of being in Zoar, and so hiding away becomes his mode of operation and, by extension, the mode of operation for his daughters.

While there is something to be said about the daughters' hope for a future, in a manner not entirely unlike Sarah's earlier action toward Hagar, the daughters' circumstances pose a tension in the narrative that must be attended to. There is a complex tension here between God's unfolding a future in the face of barrenness, and human beings' undertaking a future in the face of their limited vision. Part of the immediate complexity here is not only the reality of humans possibly usurping divine initiative, but also the question of how God functions in this world, and what instruments God chooses for God's purposes. Naturally, God uses humans as instruments for God's intent and purpose for the world, but God's uses and our plans are not always immediately apparent. Discernment becomes an issue of important proportions. The daughters of Lot have in mind, and in their understandably limited vision, a future of no prospects. The narrative is interested neither in the details of the events nor in Lot's response or questions about the daughters' pregnancies, which later must clearly have been evident to Lot. Both daughters plan and participate, and imagine that only in an intoxicated state would they be able to have sex with Lot (Gen 19:33–36). In both instances, Lot is unaware of what has transpired.

We cannot miss the irony of these events. First Lot, who had the earlier opportunity to give direction and to protect the future of his daughters, instead sacrifices them, and thereby relinquishes his responsibility and control. Here, by his daughters' actions, Lot will unwittingly provide for the future of his daughters without being in control. Second, the narrator is intentional in making known to us that "Lot did not know when she lay down or when she rose" (Gen 19:33, 35). Again, unwittingly Lot did "know" his daughters, though he did not "know" of their actions. Moreover, if Lot is indeed righteous and should be envisioning the future of those who are dependent on him, then perhaps Lot's actions of giving his daughters to violent men in Sodom and Gomorrah also have implications for his daughters' understanding of and confidence in God's shaping their fortune. While hardly a justification for the daughters' actions, nonetheless Lot's giving his daughters to the cities' violent men is something of an explanation, for the forces of actions that seek to end states of barrenness. Thus, not only did the barrenness of the daughters' future loom into their consciousness; but perhaps, in acting as they did, Lot's daughters not only fulfilled their quest but also then set into motion events and relationships that would underlie and complicate nations and states.

THE ANXIETY OF ABRAHAM AND OF SARAH (GENESIS 15–16)

In the face of barrenness, patience and hope potentially become casualties. In Genesis 15, God assures Abraham: it is the Other, God, who is called into question. Given that God offers no timeline with the promise, as Abraham and Sarah continue to grow older, with no sign of either physical barrenness ending or the promise being fulfilled, Abraham becomes anxious. We should keep in mind that neither Abraham's anxiety about the promise nor Sarah's actions later in using Hagar should necessarily and entirely be construed to signal a lack of their faith. Both Abraham and Sarah believed in the promise made to them. I would suggest that the anxiety and wondering are borne as much out of their belief as anything. Indeed they so much believed in God's promises that as time drifted, they wandered.

In Genesis 15, the fundamental issue is patience in the Other. This chapter is an exercise in patience, as God does not give Abraham any timelines. While it surely takes a degree of courage and faith to believe even when there is a timeline, a promise without a timeline compels humans to believe in that over which they have no control. It is not an uncommon occurrence to have divine promises or pronouncements without a timeline. In the New Testament, one of the most misunderstood and misused idea surrounds the timeline of Jesus's second coming. Over time, through a combination of intrigue and curiosity, control and impatience some have sought to determine a date and time of Jesus's return and to reconfigure such information as a commercial venture—making "bets" on Christ's return. While Abraham has no such entrepreneurial inclination, he is nonetheless wondering, a wondering that is evidently borne out of his conviction that enough time has elapsed, and nothing has transpired. God's response to Abraham is enveloped in two central ideas, both of which, I believe, have implications for us. First, "do not be afraid" (Gen 16:1).

It is a greeting that presupposes an element of fear, perhaps more than likely a fear justified. With this act of greeting, God acknowledges that fear is not a matter of faithlessness, but a human phenomenon that is intimately tied to hope unrealized, hope for a future that seemed for a while impossible to imagine. We can think of the assurance given to the shepherds in the field as they are told of "this thing" that has happened and of their role (Luke 2:10); or Mary, justifiably fearful, greeted and assured by the angel, with the words, "do not be afraid" (Luke 1:30). Fright is a natural human tendency particularly in circumstances over which we have little or no control. Moreover, we are reminded that promises from God (not necessarily those that are narrowly tied to timelines) are what lead us forward. It is a further reminder to Abraham that this promise that will end the barrenness of their lives does not come with a "when." This is an understanding in the narrative—as neither God nor Abraham broaches this subject in the first place, and, in fact, the journey begins without a "when." God's assurance to Abraham is that Abraham's vision of his own future is moving in a direction that God does not intend. What Abraham wonders about regarding the future is what Abraham is able to see. What Abraham sees is a "slave" as an "heir"; what God sees and promises is a "son" as an heir (Gen 15:3). The issue here is patience in a promise—that the promise maker will fulfill the promise.

Second, in all that God says to Abraham, there is essentially no new element to the promise. This is no "new and improved" promise—it is simply an abbreviated form of the same promise. This reiteration of an old promise flies in the face of churches and societies often confronted with a culture of material possessions that come with promises that continue to exceed all that has been said. Often, for a product to continue to hold the attention of the consumer, new promises about its potential and possibilities must be made. So if Abraham can believe that God scattered the stars in the sky, then he will have to believe that God will indeed fulfill the promise in God's own time.

As if to underline the difficulty of waiting, there is a sense in which Sarah takes the action of waiting even further than Abraham does. She had waited long enough, in her estimation, with no sign of her physical barrenness transforming; like Abraham, she could only see immediately before her. If Abraham seems impatient with the *Other*, then Sarah adds further to this by using the *other* (Hagar) to fulfill God's promise (Gen 16:2). Like Abraham, Sarah believed in the promise, but by Genesis 16, she has come to two conclusions: she would not be the bearer of Abraham's son, and she would have to make a life sacrifice to fulfill the promise. We are reminded that neither of these factors was part of God's promise. Despite her faith, Sarah has, in a manner, come to a point of resignation. Her use of Hagar to fulfill the promise of a future, as she understands it, is not negotiated, discussed, or requested, drawing a parallel of God's call to them where there is no discussion or negotiation. In terms of the acceptable legal protocol of the ancient Near East (cf., the *Code of Hammurabi*), what Sarah chooses to do is perfectly acceptable, legally. Yet, her actions cannot be understood from this perspective. Sarah takes a step from which there is no point of return. Like the measures that Lot's daughters took to secure their futures, Sarah's actions have extraordinary ripple effects. Whereas what Sarah did might have been legally within the acceptable boundaries, in giving Hagar to Abraham, Sarah skirts the issue of trust and confidence in the Other. Sarah's faith has not finally found a way of believing that her personal barrenness and the prospects for a barren future could be transformed. Hope for an open future has given way to a time of set boundaries. Sarah's acknowledgement that God has prevented her from having children (Gen 16:2) underlies her actions, and grounds her feelings that God has also chosen not to remove her barrenness.

Sarah sees God's promise as indeed involving her, but now concludes that the only way of fulfilling the promise would be to acknowledge the permanence of her barrenness, and have the experience of a child through someone else. The challenge that Sarah faces is one that confronts most of us who imagine after a while that whatever state of barrenness we find ourselves in will likely remain forever. Abraham, who himself was assured, does not object to Sarah's proposition, and together they allow their actions to suggest the end of their hope for God's initiative. Instead of remembering the voice of God, Abraham listened to the voice of Sarah. We might think of Abraham and Sarah's course of action as a barrenness of hope in the face of physical barrenness. Sarah's vision is dimmed and bounded by her incapacity to see beyond her own finitude. Abraham's silence resounds in sharpness, particularly in juxtaposition both to the imposed silence of Hagar and to the silencing of the voice of God, the one who would fulfill the promise.

BARRENNESS OF CONFIDENCE IN THE *OTHER* (GENESIS 20)

By the narrator's own description, Abraham is but a sojourner in Gerar (Gen 20:1)—an outsider who, by definition, depends on the hospitality of the people of Gerar. Yet, his immediate point of reference is one of distrust of the "other," and this distrust has in turn quite particular and direct consequences for Abimelech. It is Abraham's personal "barrenness" in his view of the "other" that shapes his decision to focus entirely on his personal well-being and safety at the expense of the "other." Further, such barrenness of trust sacrifices both Sarah's present and the future prospect for an heir. By sacrificing Sarah as his "sister," Abraham allows Sarah's future as the mother of the promise to be endangered, and thus endangers the future of the promise. In seeking to protect himself (v. 11), Abraham neglects those around him and makes a request of Sarah that sacrifices her (v. 2). Abraham's barrenness in his approach to the "other" is forged out of distrust and a technical truth (vv. 11–12), neither of which bodes well for the promise of a future.

For the sake of protecting the present and the promise of the future, God intervenes; though in a somewhat surprising turn of events, it is Abimelech, the king of Gerar, whom God addresses (vv. 3–8). Again, as we have witnessed in God's encounter with Hagar, God gives a voice to the "other" that Abraham has cast aside. In the case of Abimelech, the narrator invites us to see the unintended consequences of a barrenness that is self-consumed. It is true that in asking Sarah to be his "sister," Abraham is using a "truth" as it fits with his plans. As we might easily surmise here, a technical truth will not suffice for his own protection. By his actions, Abraham literally endangers the life of Abimelech and the people of Gerar. Death is on the threshold, and Abraham is unaware of the consequences of his actions. Perhaps it is the case here that Abraham will have to face the nature of his barrenness through the confrontation or challenge of the "other." It is Abimelech, not God, who confronts Abraham, and Abraham both explains and seeks to justify his actions, though it is clear to us that his actions are not justifiable. But neither God nor Abimelech pronounces punishment of Abraham, and thus even though Abraham recompenses greatly, he is also left to find himself in his state of barrenness.

The intent of this episode is not to resolve Abraham's barrenness. The intent of this episode is rather to introduce us to the further consequences of this state of barrenness and to the effects of Abraham's distrusting not only the "other" but also God's unfolding of a future. Moreover, it is Abimelech who engages God on this occasion on behalf of the innocent. Reminiscent of Abraham's questioning God on behalf of Sodom and Gomorrah (Gen 18:23–33), Abimelech asks God, "Lord, will you destroy an innocent people?" (Gen 20:4). It is to God's justice that Abimelech appeals, and not to his personal innocence in the matter. Aware of Abimelech's pureness of heart and his integrity, God spares the king and the people from death. Enough textual evidence suggests that Abimelech, like others before, pleads before God for his own innocence. Moreover Abimelech has an understanding and vision that Abraham does not appear to have or to employ. Whereas God tells Abimelech that he himself is the one who faces death, Abimelech understands that both his actions and God's pronouncement of punishment will not affect him personally, but rather the people of Gerar. This he understands instinctively. While the narrative attributes to Abimelech a barrenness of sorts, Abimelech is the one, after all, who acts with integrity of heart and with innocence; and more important, God is aware of this (Gen 20:5–6). God does not share Abraham's barrenness of trust in the "other," yet God makes clear that Abimelech is the one who must make amends (v. 7).

With all of his frailties and flaws, Abraham remains nonetheless God's servant, the one set apart for God's future purpose. This episode reinforces for us the reality that often God not only begins from a point of barrenness but also often continues to use those in states of barrenness to fulfill God's promises. Even though God does not directly communicate with Abraham, Abraham is nevertheless made to face his actions. Abimelech's questions are profoundly human questions; questions that seek to understand why we do what we do; questions that wonder aloud, what could possibly have prompted one to cause another such pain, and to bring such guilt? (vv. 9–10).

But these are neither rhetorical questions nor questions to determine what actions should be taken. Rather Abimelech's questions are more for Abraham's self-examination, and indeed Abraham does answer. Abraham's answers, typical of human responses to questions that challenge the self, combine rationalization, explanation, and justification. Abraham's personal barrenness, shaped by fear of the "other," emerges here more fully as he acknowledges his perception that "fear of God," causes him to call Sarah his sister. Indeed, Abraham shows us fear over Sarah's welfare; and by appearing to Abimelech in a vision, God answers Abraham's perception that Abimelech and his people lack the fear of God. Following on God's admonition, Abimelech does not respond to Abraham's explanation and justification (vv. 11–13). It is Sarah to whom Abimelech grants a form of recompense and a complete vindication. Striking here is that in addressing Sarah, Abimelech refers to Abraham as her "brother" (Gen 20:16). If for no other reason than she is technically Abraham's sister, Sarah is not made to be culpable, nor does Abimelech lead her to realize that he is aware of her marginal and coerced complicity in Abraham's plan.

At the end of the episode, to be sure, Abraham continues on the journey virtually unscathed, though we can never be certain that Sarah is not wounded. Moreover, the narrative is not particularly interested in telling us whether Abraham's view of the "other" is transformed by this event. We are reminded in Genesis 20:13 that Abraham asks Sarah to say at every place that she is his sister. Whether this happened in every instance we are unsure. Perhaps it is the case that Abraham felt that the weight of the promise depended on him, and thus he was the one to be protected at all costs. Equally possible is that God will continue to remind us that God will use whomever God chooses— indeed including someone like Abraham, who is willing to sacrifice the promise because of his own barrenness of trust.

Of striking and perhaps worrisome significance in this episode are the consequences of one's barrenness for others, and particularly for the innocent. We cannot miss the connection between Abraham's barrenness (in terms of his lack of trust), which not only endangers the life of one person but also imperils an entire community, and the divinely cast state of barrenness on the king's entire household of women, including the female slaves. Moreover, an essential component of the threefold promise made to Abraham in Genesis 12:1–4 is the promise of being a blessing to others, as he has received a blessing from God. At least in the very initial stages, Abraham's actions are more of a curse than a blessing, and indeed this component of the divine promise is virtually absent from both Abraham's thoughts and actions.

In focusing exclusively on *his* concerns and needs, Abraham not only sacrifices and endangers Sarah and the promise of an heir, but also he becomes more of a curse than a blessing to the "other." It is God's intervention with the "other" that undoes the curse and brings goodness and blessings. On account of Sarah's sacrifice, the most vulnerable and powerful pay a price. To be sure, whereas Abraham's actions are seen as instrumental, God's action in punishing the innocent causes us to wonder about both the nature and the extent of the punishment. If this action of God leaves us wondering, then perhaps so does the fact that God undoes not only the punishment but also the plans for punishment. Thus, the reality is that in the face of actions that brought Abimelech to the brink of death, God retracts God's pronouncement and God's plans for death. Out of death comes life, not only in the present, but also now for the future. The possibility for progeny not only comes to the powerful but also to the powerless. Indeed, the promise for a future is directed not only to those on the "inside," but also to those who are on the margin. The God of barren Abraham and barren Sarah is the God of the "other," and the God who spans the spectrum of creation.

2

THE CHALLENGE OF
WILDERNESS

FLEEING TO THE WILDERNESS FOR LIFE
(GENESIS 16)

HUMAN ABANDONMENT IS matched by divine care, and within the
Bible, divine care often occurs in the context of the wilderness. This
"hostile" environment of the wilderness stands in sharp contrast to
the "hospitable" environment of Sarah and Abraham's household.
Hagar is the one who is afflicted with challenges, and who overturns
the conventions and natural order of things.

The silence of the text about the hardships of a pregnant woman,
alone, underlines Hagar's devastating predicament in the wilderness.
Sarah and Abraham's abandonment is sharply juxtaposed to the divine
initiative, care, and promise. Casting Hagar away allows Abraham to
"wash his hands" and Sarah to erase her presence. In Sarah's eyes,
Hagar has come between herself and Abraham. After Sarah has mal-
treated, abused, and finally dismissed her, the pregnant Hagar sees the
wilderness and the likely prospect of death as a viable alternative to
her present misery. With this choice, Hagar is understood to be gone,
essentially banished from Sarah's life.

The wilderness experience signals a new beginning for Hagar.
Despite Abraham and Sarah's plan to exile her, the reality is that they
will have to reckon with Hagar's new beginning, and indeed their

very household will be the environment for Hagar's newness. From the shelter of a home to the harshness of the wilderness, the narrative assures us that God will function in any and all settings, environments, and circumstances. Where and how God will act, how God will make God's presence known is not dependent on the structures and constriction created and concretized by humans. Among the many reminders of God's encounter with Hagar in the wilderness is the distinct reality that before all things, God is a Creator God, who is not to be narrowly defined, or (worse) owned. The wilderness, like any other place, is where one may encounter the divine; with a divine word, any place becomes a threshold for new beginnings. Moreover, as in the case Abraham and Sarah, it is entirely possible that God uses persons despite themselves.

Both the voicelessness and anonymity of Hagar are removed in and through the wilderness experience with God. Unlike Sarah, who waited and waited for God's attention to her barrenness, Hagar is immediately met by God's angel and has a ready and unexpected conversation with God (Gen 16:7–13). This encounter further separates Hagar from Sarah and in fact places Hagar in fairly select company. One cannot overlook the drama of such an encounter, as Hagar is without any credential for such a ready meeting with the God of Abraham and Sarah. Indeed, it is only in the wilderness that Hagar finally has a voice. One cannot miss the irony here, given that the wilderness is one of the last places where one is likely to be heard from or, for that matter, spoken to. Yet, away from the human environment, Hagar is granted a voice, is spoken to, and is heard.

Hagar is never allowed to have a voice before, during, or after the birth of Ishmael. Both naming and voice come to Hagar away from the "hospitable" environs of a household and in the shared but uncharted territory of the wilderness. The "owned" and "protected" space of Abraham and Sarah does not allow the outsider to enter; but it is God's open and shared space—desolate and difficult as it is—that allows voice, and thus belonging. The "open" and "free" space of the wilderness, in fact, protects Hagar. From the outset, the narrator alerts us to the prospect of life. Life is certainly not what we would immediately associate with wilderness, and yet the encounter between Hagar and the angel takes place by a spring of water (Gen 16:7). How Hagar finds her way here, or is led here, we are not told. Clearly the point is not how Hagar came to be at the spring in the wilderness; rather the narrative immediately highlights the reality that the spring is the essence of life's sustenance. Before Hagar receives a voice and before God establishes her identity, the gift of life is present. Perhaps the presence of life here invites us to imagine that the wilderness will provide life beyond what is known about and associated with the wilderness. Here as elsewhere, the divine does what the human protectors fail to do. While for Abraham and Sarah, the wilderness lies beyond the scope of habitation and belonging, the landscape of God's activity is limitless, and the theophany of Genesis 16 is not only an invitation for Hagar but also an invitation to Abraham and Sarah to envision and know God as Creator God.

Despite Hagar's fleeing into the wilderness, the angel of God makes clear that her identity is inextricably tied to Sarah's identity (v. 9). In making this pronouncement, the narrator allows neither Sarah nor Hagar to query or argue. Hagar's survival and the survival of her son will be in the shadow of Sarah and her household, and Sarah's future and the future of her son will forever be shaped by Hagar and her son. The premier element that the angel's question generates is that Hagar does have an identity, and it is tied to Sarah—it is Sarah from whom she comes, and Sarah to whom she will return. Thus the one who flees for fear of harshness must reconcile for the sake of her future. Such a framework is brokered in the wilderness. Hagar's return to Sarah's household also establishes a new understanding of power and a new alignment of such power. On the surface, Hagar's matter-of-fact return to Sarah and Abraham's household might naturally imply a return to the status quo. Yet of course we know it is not, for Hagar is returning with a source of divine power. Both covenant bearers and servants, insiders and outsiders, will be guided by the same source of power, without human constraints.

It is Hagar's silent response (now that she has a voice) that is most remarkable here. She neither challenges nor questions nor rejects the pronouncement of this unknown God. Hagar's response should not be underestimated in its import since she places considerable trust in this God, whom she has only now encountered. Moreover, she returns to Abraham and Sarah's household with a new level of trust in the future. She returns from the wilderness with a promise (Gen 16:11–12). Neither Sarah nor Abraham is aware at this point of the nature of the promise and of the future that it brings.

In many parts of the world, one is often defined by what one owns and by the material possessions that one has. In this instance, while Hagar lacks both ownership and material possessions, she returns with something that cannot be immediately realized, yet with something that holds the key—indeed with something that *is* the key—to the future. Even the displaced will have a future, born out of suffering and exile. While it is virtually impossible to gauge the level or quality of faith evidenced by Sarah and Abraham, and by Hagar, it seems, purely on the basis of Hagar's acceptance of the angel's message (particularly in the face of her experience in Sarah's household) that Hagar's faith is at least as striking as the faith of Abraham and Sarah, and is in its own way remarkable. The significance of the narrator's choice in this episode to juxtapose the household of Sarah and Abraham to the wilderness cannot be overstated. The contrast between belonging and outcast; between shelter and harshness; between hope and despair; between, on the one hand, the promise of newness and, on the other hand, the bleakness of both the present and the future are all captured in this juxtaposition. Yet, newness will come in the harshness of the present, and the prospect of a fragile child will be confirmed precisely in the rough and harsh wilderness.

Like Sarah, however, Hagar will have to wait and be patient for the right time, and the promise within the wilderness will be realized in the inhospitable confines of Sarah and Abraham's household. This waiting will not be routinely easy, as Hagar's silence perhaps testifies. Hagar runs away from Sarah's household in fear because of the harsh treatment; and she returns, perhaps still in fear, and certainly as servant, but aware of a new reality that cannot be dismissed as issuing from contempt. Just as we had no indication of Hagar's voice with Abraham and Sarah before she fled to the wilderness, so also we have no indication that upon her return she has a voice in Sarah's house. Identity in the household of Sarah will not be shaped by voice.

The angel's question to Hagar is, "Hagar, slave-girl of Sarah, where have you come from and where are you going?" (v. 7). Thus, two issues frame Hagar's identity. The particularity of the question posed to Hagar has universal implications. In the first place, the narrator invites readers to view the spectrum of life as a journey. Always thus, using the journey motif, one's identity is shaped by the past, present, and future. In the case of Hagar, her response to the angel's question is telling. That the narrator has the angel ask such a question might suggest that within the narrative, the angel's encounter with Hagar is a "fact-finding mission"; but for Hagar, the angelic encounter *elicits her own acknowledgement of* her identity.

Hagar's response to the angel reflects two important factors about her situation. First, Hagar is "running from"—escaping—from her past: not the past that she has chosen, but one that has been imposed on her. Nonetheless, it is not that she is "running to," but that she is "running from." Perhaps this is one of the narrator's reasons for establishing that Hagar must return to her past—in this case, to a painful past. The underlying suggestion here is that one cannot run from one's past. This is not to suggest that one must dwell there permanently, but it is to suggest that one's future is invariably, inextricably tied to and shaped by the landscape of one's past. There might likely be temporary respite as one "runs from," but, finally, the narrative invites a conscious acknowledgment that running from one's past is not a viable option.

Second, whereas the angel's question is bracketed by "from" and "to," Hagar's response focuses sharply and entirely on "from." Her present is precarious, and her future is unknown; she does not venture a response about her future. The angel neither seeks nor receives an explanation from Hagar about the future. The angel's response is exact and, on the surface, unyielding: "Return . . . and submit" (Gen 16:9). Hagar's present will continue in a manner that is aggressive. While the promise of a child points to the future, this future will be born out of a presence that is shaped by the persistent and patient role of servant. Hagar is to submit. This is certainly difficult to comprehend, let alone to accept. As readers, we are naturally prompted to ask, "But why?" Why send Hagar into such a household where, justified or not on Sarah's part, there is harshness? Yet, here it is. Hagar is to submit; she is to face her circumstances. As if to establish clearly that Hagar's past will not become her present and will not continue changeless into her future, the angel announces Hagar's future—a future certainly, unknown to Hagar until this point. Hagar's future will be carried in her heart.

Even as Hagar's earlier answer focused entirely on her past, so now the angel's words will begin to shape the other end of her journey's spectrum, which lies beyond the past. This promise reaches way beyond Hagar's capacity. Just as the specter of the wilderness first pointed to death and yet, for Hagar, unexpectedly and startlingly brought life (i.e., water, divine presence, promise), perhaps the promise of descendants beyond reckoning, even more than the birth of life out of death, will stretch Hagar's imagination. The future is embodied in Hagar, and yet the future promised to and through her will never be fully realized in her time. She will have to trust.

At some external level, it appears that Sarah and Hagar both have a yet-to-be-determined future over which they have little control. Yet, the parallels and congruences separate in marked ways. To be sure, Sarah's barrenness must be reckoned with as lying beyond her control. In this regard, she will have to trust in the divine promise. But as we have seen, Sarah has power to act on her own behalf (her misguided use of power over Hagar leads to seriously devastating effects). Hagar, however, has no such power; her promise for a future lies in the power of God, and she understands this. Moreover, it seems that it is inconceivable to have a divine encounter in the wilderness and not believe. The wilderness, for Hagar, is her point of departure for trust. For good or ill, she has no power to act independently, and as if to intensify further this reality of dependence, she is made to return to live in Sarah's household. Like the "how" of the promise God made to Sarah, the "how" of God's promise to Hagar will only be realized in God's time. The issue of Hagar's returning to Sarah and submitting to her is problematic for readers. Because the demand for Hagar to submit comes as a divine imperative, there has been and continues to be a tendency either to justify such a pronouncement or to view it with a quality of merit. Personally, I find myself as one such reader, but my struggle with such an understanding or explanation continues, as I find neither option remotely satisfactory. It is certainly not to "second guess" God as it is to wonder without necessarily settling too readily for an understanding.

While clearly a promise for future life is granted to Hagar (indeed one that parallels to a degree the promise to Abraham and Sarah), the promise to Hagar is nonetheless not without the prospect of future conflict (Gen 16:12). As Sarah waits, now with the unanticipated additional burden of her action to fulfill the promise of an heir through Hagar, Hagar is granted the further divine investment in her future through the naming of her son (Gen 16:11). The continued revelation of God as one who acts in every place, bringing life in the midst of death is clearly demonstrated. It is in the wilderness that the naming takes place, and in naming comes belonging.

We cannot overlook or miss the proposed significance of God's naming Ishmael—hardly a routine occurrence in the Bible. While the granting of the name from God is directly in particularly to Hagar, as in the ongoing encounter between God and Hagar in the wilderness, the implications of the naming have greater breadth beyond the immediate moment. God listens to the cries of those who are in a wilderness, particularly, as is typical, where there is a sense of hopelessness. What is given to Hagar thus is promise to all. Like Sarah, Hagar thus embodies that for which many of us long and hope: promise, hope, freedom, belonging, future. Hagar's wilderness experience invites us to enter her story and, in the way of and with the depth of a myth, allows her story to become our story. It is very clear why Hagar's son is named Ishmael: the Lord has listened to her affliction (Gen 16:11). This is, I believe, an instructive statement, in that the divine action at our level does not necessarily seem to have a natural connection to Hagar's affliction.

The themes of present reality and future promise merge, and, indeed, in the promise God pronounces the two to be connected. In fact, the promise suggests that in some respects present reality and future promise are inseparable. There is a precise and active conversation between the two. However, at least in the instance of Genesis 16, an unstated note indicates a somewhat marked variation for expressing divine and human attention to matters of affliction and oppression. Because human finitude allows finally only for a vision that is shaped by a somewhat foreseeable future, consequences (or promises, for that matter) are typically pronounced or understood with a temporal frame in our time. Yet, in Genesis 16:11, it is clear that the divine initiative is in no way limited by this life and by human time constraints.

Not only is Hagar's affliction heeded and acted upon, but also Hagar hears the language chosen, sparse as it is, without comment. This promise, which will be realized and will blossom beyond her lifetime, brings with it a new and different prospect for pain and despair. Her promised son will be "a wild ass of a man, with his hand against everyone, and everyone's hand against him; and he shall live at odds with all of his kin" (Gen 16:12). This can hardly be comforting to Hagar; a different and perhaps more extensive "wilderness" experience looms in the future. Yes, to be sure, this is a promise; but is this a solace to Hagar? Not only must she return and submit to Sarah (a very present reality), but now she carries a promise that unmistakably hints at abuse and pain of a wider and more systemic nature for the future. That which she has received at the hands of Sarah will be meted out by her descendants in a time to come, and no one will be spared.

How could this be comforting in any possible way to Hagar? I find this challenging, and an interpretation that says Hagar's descendants will have power and force in a way that she could never have is not particularly satisfying. To be sure, Ishmael will have the opportunity and circumstances to accomplish that which Hagar was unable to do and was deprived of; nevertheless, this fact alone remains unsatisfying. God is clearly the architect, but we must (indeed we are invited to) wonder at what cost Ishmael will be able to accomplish what his mother could not. One of the challenges in Genesis 16:12 is precisely the possibility of a much more pronounced cycle of violence to keep spiraling in a systemic way.

One of the lingering questions that this particular text raises for me centers on the issue of whether God initiates and creates intentionally conflictual situations. While, personally, I would like to think otherwise, the reality is that Ishmael will be a person of conflict to both kin and nonkin alike. As we continue to reflect on Hagar's experience in the wilderness, this particular component can neither be underestimated nor overlooked. The physical wilderness experience and the evident wilderness of the times in Sarah's household now are coupled with the somewhat more challenging idea of a wilderness prospect of what is within the heart; Hagar must carry the clearly painful divine words.

Hagar's response to the wilderness is remarkable in that she listens, believes, and takes the promise given to her. Equally remarkable, in my estimation, is what she does *not* do, namely challenge, refuse, walk away from, or reject God. Rather, yet again what she does places her in very select company in the life of ancient Israel. Her role in the narrative will gradually diminish, but not before a final extraordinary moment in this encounter with God in the wilderness. Hagar names God. Her naming of God—in itself remarkable in its audacious simplicity—opens for us yet a wider vision for encountering and understanding God. This is the God of Sarah and Abraham, who sees (Gen 16:13); this is a God who sees not only the needs of those at the center of power but also those who are cast away into the wilderness.

What we have in Genesis 16:11–12 are two pillars of the divine that represent human longing in a most profound way. In God's naming a son Ishmael, we know that God hears and heeds; and the human response is, in turn, to name the divine namer. God hears, God sees, God heeds. Hagar, the one who is forced to run in the wilderness and now to return to Sarah's household, is a silent witness to what is possible even in a state of wilderness: one might say particularly in a state of wilderness—a most unlikely place to encounter God, counter to human conventions. Hagar understands, in a sense, the magnitude of her experience; one does not see God and live, and yet Hagar's seeing God and remaining alive is exactly what happens, and Hagar understands this (Gen 16:13). Genesis 16:15 reminds us that while encountering God in the wilderness does usher in change, often the one encountered has to continue living in certain circumstances. So in Genesis 16:15, Hagar recedes into the narrative background after Ishmael is born.

REVISITING THE WILDERNESS AND FACING DEATH (GENESIS 21)

As Hagar's journey in Sarah's household continues upon her return from the wilderness, we are not privy to what transpires during the years after Ishmael's birth and the weaning of Isaac; the narrative is silent. As risky as it is to interpret a text from its silence, occasionally we are not only faced with what a text says, but also with what it does not say, or what is altogether absent. How was Hagar treated? Did Sarah's harshness continue? What did Hagar say to Sarah and Abraham on her return? Did Sarah understand that Hagar's return was God's mandate? How does the presence of Ishmael affect Sarah's sense of self, particularly in the absence of any divine initiative on her behalf? The questions abound, and while one cannot or must not draw definitive conclusions on textual silence, it is certainly the case that one is left to wonder about these questions. Thus, what happens in the household remains a mystery, and perhaps we may instinctively conclude that such details are not of interest to the narrator, though such a conjecture (plausible as it might be) remains unsatisfactory. What we may safely conclude is that under somewhat difficult and challenging conditions, Ishmael was born and grew up.

When the Hagar narrative resumes in Genesis 21, years have passed; and while Hagar and now Ishmael have continued in Sarah's household, we discover that with much change, much has remained unchanged. Genesis 21:1–8 establishes the scene and setting of what is to transpire in the lives of Hagar and Ishmael—the wilderness revisited under new circumstances. Within God's time, Sarah becomes pregnant, reminding us that, finally, while this is to be Abraham's son, the matter of bearing a son was about *Sarah*. Alluding to the nature of the household, verse 6 serves as an insight into Sarah's household and her state of being before the birth of her son: "'God has brought laughter for me; everyone who hears will laugh with me.'" It is with Isaac that laughter and joy have come to Sarah. She understands that it is God who, in granting her a child, has removed her physical barrenness and brought laughter to her. Her personal fulfillment in the experience of birthing a child is finally what generates this thought. Could one assume that there had been no laughter in the Sarah's household in the birthing, weaning, and growing up of Ishmael? Perhaps so. Sarah announces that everyone who hears will laugh with her.

But the truth is that *not everyone* will laugh with Sarah. It is rather *everyone* who is *anyone* in Sarah's eyes who will laugh. Hearing and laughing are together. God has heard and acted, but for Hagar, her wilderness experience continues, and there is no laughter for her. Indeed it is the underside of Sarah's laughter that ushers in Hagar's wilderness. The focus on Sarah and her miracle of bearing a son casts a shadow on Hagar and Ishmael. As if to underline and intensify this "dark side" of laughter, it is in the midst of joyous celebration (21:8) that the (but) introduces Sarah's fear and jealousy: "But Sarah saw the son of Hagar the Egyptian, whom she had borne to Abraham, playing with her son Isaac" (21:9). This is the point of transformation, perhaps the cumulative effect of Ishmael's years in Sarah's house and in the vision of Sarah and her barrenness.

As has been mentioned above, the narrative is silent about the birth and rearing of Ishmael, and so there is no implicit or explicit understanding for Sarah's immediate and somewhat urgent action of sending Hagar and Ishmael away (21:10). The very thing that has come to Sarah as a miracle, namely laughter, is precisely what the brothers are engaged in, and what leads to pain and punishment. Sarah imagines Ishmael's playing with her son as a detriment to Isaac.

As we have witnessed earlier in this book, many of us who read and study these narratives seek either to exonerate Sarah or at the very least to explain away her actions as having some legitimacy. Despite particularly some arguments along these lines, it seems to me that Sarah's actions are born out of a maternal instinct generated by an experience of barrenness that has dominated her life. Fear ungrounded becomes her point of departure for acting in such a blindingly harsh manner. Laughter, after all, is not for everyone.

Again, it is to Abraham that Sarah turns, and again he is the messenger who brings the news of banishment to Hagar and to his son. The narrative does not indicate that Sarah weighs the costs either of the fact that this is Abraham's son (*his* firstborn) or of the need to rid her house of their presence and the interminable reminder of her decision to give her servant to her husband. And thus, now the young Ishmael and Hagar must experience the wilderness again and the very real possibility of death. We cannot help but be struck here by the oft-thought-of idea that despite public harmony, and even laughter, certain groups may not live under the same roof.

Sarah's actions raise a difficult and complex issue that indeed has large and universal implications. What clearly threatens Sarah is certainly not another generation of master-slave paralleling her relationship with Hagar, but even more troubling, the fear of equality. With the possibility of equality, a brother is banished. Such fear dominated Sarah. For a while, shared space in her household was tolerable, but shared space in the life of her son proves intolerable, and Hagar and Ishmael must go. Even as Sarah makes this decision, the decision does beg the question: what does it mean to have a shared life with an outsider? Is Sarah really fearful of Isaac's inheritance? Is this enough of a reason to banish the "other": a brother, a son? For Sarah, her fear was enough of a reason. The reason for Hagar and Ishmael's banishment is certainly not so much a matter of giving Hagar and Ishmael their freedom (and thus relinquishing Ishmael's claim to inheritance) as some (e.g., Nahum Sarna) have claimed; but rather the reason for Hagar and Ishmael's banishment is a persistent fear in Sarah, one that is sharp and to the point: "Cast out this slave woman with her son" (21:10). This is not language granting freedom. It is language of banishment, of exile. Moreover as we witnessed in Genesis 16, Sarah's decision is not designed for negotiation; this is an imperative. Neither in Genesis 16 nor here (Gen 21:10) is there any indication that Sarah takes Abraham into account as Ishmael's father, and in both instances there is self-imposed silence by Abraham.

Yet, despite Abraham's silence, the narrator is clear about the effect of Sarah's decision on Abraham. Abraham is very distressed about his son and what is about to transpire (Gen 21:11). Hagar and Ishmael will literally be cast into the wilderness, but Abraham (in a different way) will face his own wilderness—the loss of a son, his first-born son. Here the issue is not about inheritance and fear of equality. For surely in the eyes of Abraham, the father of both Ishmael and Isaac, there can be no other option but equality and shared space. Further, as we saw in Genesis 16, God hears and sees the distressed. But again, as in Genesis 16:9, it seems that God's response to Abraham is equally distressing. How could casting away Hagar and Ishmael be proper or decent? Yet, God tells Abraham to listen to what Sarah has decided.

For Abraham's personal wilderness perhaps blinds him to the minimal nature of sustenance that he provides for Hagar and Ishmael. The meager provisions of Abraham will stand in sharp contrast to the divine provisions in the wilderness. So as the dawn breaks, Abraham bids farewell to Hagar and his son; they leave to enter their darkness, a final disappearance from his life. There will no longer be a shared space, and yet there is no space where Hagar and Ishmael can go. Yet again, Hagar becomes a wanderer. Just as Sarah's harshness in Genesis 16:6 ('nh) alludes intertextually to the harshness that the Israelites suffer at the hands of the Egyptian task masters (Exod 1:11–14), so also Genesis 21 (Hagar's departure from her house of bondage to find herself wandering) alludes to the descendants of Abraham and Sarah, who will leave their bondage to wander in the wilderness. Perhaps worse than the later Israelites, Hagar and Ishmael wander in a state of uncertainty (t'h) with no particular destination (Gen 21:14). Moreover, as we discover, divine provision comes without Hagar's complaint or murmuring; God provides, as God would do for the Israelites later (Gen 21:17–20).

Elsewhere I have suggested that when a person or a people is in exile, death might very well manifest itself in a variety of ways. Certainly there is the most evident and obvious way for death to show itself, namely the loss of one's land, one's literal sense of place. Restricted as Hagar's place was, she certainly experienced this loss. Whatever other security a person needs, it seems that one must begin with physical security, a place of physical belonging, a place of shelter. In this very basic way, then, Hagar experiences profound loss. But for her, the wilderness experience, her exile, will have several other devastating branches. Whatever secondary community she might have called her own is now removed, and thus she is twice removed from a belonging community. Moreover, while the narrative is silent on the issue of what Hagar might be thinking regarding the God of Abraham and Sarah (whom she has now seen and heard), surely there must be some wondering about why this second wilderness experience has begun.[1]

As if this were not enough, Hagar is faced with the prospect of witnessing the death of her son, the death of a promise, the death of a hope, and perhaps the death of a newly found faith in the God of Abraham and Sarah. Not surprisingly the end of the water hints at the first sign of death: "she cast the child under one of the bushes" (21:15). A simple reading of this verse in the larger context of this narrative causes readers to experience a constriction of breath, for there seems to be an ongoing, relentless move towards death. Maybe this is a sign that there is very little that Hagar can do for her son, and this movement away from him at least physically distances her from her son.

1. See Gossai, *Power and Marginality*.

One of the unresolvable issues here certainly has to do with which alternative is preferable: to watch a child die or to close one's eyes. I find neither alternative particularly appealing, and the very idea of the death of one's child is so gut wrenching as to be unfathomable to me. More to the point of Hagar's choice, I cannot imagine it. Yet, it seems to me that this choice is precisely one issue that we must struggle with. Having been tormented by the choice that Sophie makes in William Styron's *Sophie's Choice*, and by the depth of my own incapacity for understanding and incapacity for fathoming such an action, Hagar's action simply reminds me that grief, courage, selflessness, and hopelessness mingled together would be an emotional state of great magnitude. Hagar casts off (*vattashlek*) Ishmael (Gen 21:15) in a way not unlike the way Pharaoh's edict demands Israelite women to cast off all newborn boys in the Nile (Exod 1:15–16); in both cases, the same Hebrew verb is employed. Like Pharaoh's intention, Hagar's expectation must surely be death.

Hagar's own lamentation invites us to understand the emotive sense of resignation that enfolds her. The final reality for Hagar is that she cannot bear the thought of watching her child die (Gen 21:16). We are left to wonder to whom Hagar must address her lamentation. Under different circumstances, we may in fact be left to wonder, but clearly, given what we know of the silence and indeed voicelessness of Hagar, she addresses her feelings to God. It is God who had heard her in the first place, and sees her. Phyllis Trible captures, I believe, the deep affectation and poignancy of Hagar's experience: "Her grief, like her speech is sufficient unto itself. She does not cry out to another; she does not beseech God. A Madonna alone with her dying child, Hagar weeps."[2]

What is one to do in the face of the death of one's child and with the prospects of emptiness in the wilderness until one dies? Hagar knows. She knows that there is no one to turn to, and that death lurks. What is this love-broken mother to do but to join those who have gone before her, and those who would follow, in lifting up her voice and weeping? And so Hagar does precisely this, and in the simple wonder of such an act, God again hears the voice of the voiceless. On the surface, this moment appears somewhat confusing in that Hagar weeps,

2. Trible, *Texts of Terror*, 25.

but it is the voice of Ishmael that is heard. Perhaps one is left to wonder how this could be; I believe that this simple, serious, mysterious state-ment ("God again hears the voice of the voiceless.") serves as a striking reminder of the nature of this God. God listens to the voiceless.

Even in her weak and heavy-laden state, Hagar is able to raise her voice for both herself and her son. The one with a voice must cry out and weep for those who cannot. It is, I believe, entirely too easy to conclude that God overlooks Hagar and focuses on Ishmael since the narrative indicates that "God heard the voice of the boy" (Gen 21:17). For anyone and everyone who wonders where God might be in their circumstances, Genesis 21:17b becomes a critical testimony to the manner in which God functions: "'God has heard the voice of the boy where he is.'" To cast this somewhat in a more common vernacular, "God meets us where we are." The venue here for the divine-human encounter is neither narrowly prescribed nor constricted. Not only is this statement a particular reference to the wilderness or to where Ishmael is in the wilderness, but rather this statement resounds with universal implications. The drama of being close to death, of being without basic sustenance, without shelter, without a place of belong-ing, without community, in exile: this indeed is the larger context of God meeting us where we are. In the midst of such gravity, these are words of extraordinary grace. God will do the traveling to meet us in our state of being or location. God speaks for the all voiceless, includ-ing for Hagar and her son.

Hagar's actions stand in sharp contrast to those of Abraham and Sarah. Despite the seemingly odd (even insensitive) question with which the angel of God greets Hagar, again it is the case that in the midst of her wilderness experience, Hagar is invited to have a voice and to speak for herself. The angel's question and the pronouncement recognize Hagar's straits, and indeed there is no recorded answer from Hagar. Something troubles Hagar; it is not a question to elicit informa-tion regarding her state of being—she is troubled and is provided the occasion to be heard. Indeed, it is clear that her voice is Ishmael's; for him to be heard, she must be heard, and God does hear Hagar. When God speaks to Hagar (Gen 17:21), God speaks in the way that God spoke to Abraham, in the way that the angel spoke to Mary or to the shepherds. "Do not be afraid" not only recognizes fear but reason for fear. What reasons are there? One reason for fear is wilderness, and everything conjured up in one's vision and experience of wilderness. Moreover, there is fear of the unknown, fear of a lost promise, fear of death. Thus, while it is the case that a greeting such as, "do not be afraid" is rarely used today in the manner in which the angel speaks to Hagar, nonetheless it has its place in contemporary life. From a parent to a child, "do not be afraid" may have the force of bringing into reality something that appears impossible, or, conversely, of staving off that which appears to bring impending danger, pain, or doom.

I recall a Holocaust survivor, Alexander Rosner, telling the story of himself as a ten-year-old boy standing by his father's side and being confronted by an SS soldier. As the young boy trembled at the terror generated by the Nazi's voice, he squeezed the father's hand, and in one of those moments that would shape his life, his father whispered to him, "Don't be afraid." Of course there was much to be afraid of, and in fact the father's words could not and would not erase the horror to come. But in a moment of such fear and uncertainty, these words were words of grace and power.

The difference between divine and human assurance reflects both power and prescience. To Hagar and Ishmael, "Do not be afraid" are words of such force and power as to be enough. No details are spilled, and for many of us who long for hints of specific assurances, the text's concealment of so much is a reminder of the challenge of "do not be afraid." God would not allow Hagar to discard or cast away the promise; God takes immediate action to save the boy, to make him well. Most certainly the last thing on Hagar's mind is future generations. For surely, in the face of imminent death, water becomes the most urgent and immediate life resource.

As we witnessed in Genesis 16, an encounter with God brings a quality of new vision previously unknown. Hagar could see as mortals see, but it is God who could *pro-vide* (i.e., "see that which lies beyond") way beyond the human horizon. And so it is in the midst of the wilderness, where death lurks and is expected, life comes and a promise that seemed for a while to wither, is reiterated.

THE WILDERNESS OF LOT'S DAUGHTERS
(GENESIS 19)

As we saw briefly in chapter 1, the daughters of Lot face a quality of barrenness unlike Sarah and Rebekah's. While they are not physically barren, the prospects for their future cause them to envision nothing but a drying up of their heritage. The convention based on Genesis 19 is that among other things, the daughters of Lot are saved. It is almost never the case that we wonder as we read this narrative: *saved for what purpose*? Indeed, as self-evidently miserable as their circumstances appear, we might very well ask: *saved from what*? There seems to be very little doubt that the principal focus of this narrative is Lot. To the point of the daughter's decision to be impregnated by their father, choices and decisions impinge upon or surround Lot. Thus, in Genesis 19:19, it is his life, his future, and the prospects of his death that consume Lot. It is to save his own life that he pleads. As I have noted in chapter 1, it is nearly impossible to make a widely accepted case for the actions of Lot's daughters. Yet, this section of Genesis 19 refuses to be dismissed casually, or reduced to a footnote of the daughters' despicable behavior.

I would submit that in Genesis 19, the daughters of Lot find themselves in two different (though connected) states of wilderness. In the first instance, the daughters are sacrificed and abandoned by their father in one motion (Gen 19:8). As difficult as it might be to accept in the case of Hagar, given her status as slave, we might come to expect that in the household of Sarah and Abraham, she would likely find protection or at least an upholding of her sense of personhood. But here, we have the *daughters* of Lot, and there is both sacrifice and abandonment. In the household of their father Lot, they are without voice. In a moment of crisis, Lot is the one who makes a critical determination that his daughters must be sacrificed. The wilderness experience of the daughters in their father's house is as devastating as being cast into the physical, inhospitable wilderness, as Hagar was. In one's parents' house comes an expectation of physical protection, and Lot does not hint at any consideration of protecting his daughters. Indeed, in offering his daughters to the violent men of the city, he expresses no concern for their future. If, in fact, the daughters are already betrothed (implied in Genesis 19:14), Lot has made a further mockery of their future by sacrificing them as sexual objects to violent men.

It is in this state of wilderness, where all of the physical evidence should suggest otherwise, that the daughters have likely determined quietly (the only way available to them) that *they* would have to give shape and give expression to their own future. The narrative often defends Lot's actions at the daughters' expense. As important as the theme of hospitality is in this narrative, to accentuate it further than is morally acceptable, and at the expense of the marginalized and vulnerable, becomes in itself disgraceful. As challenging as it is, this first instance of the daughters' wilderness invites us to enter into their story.

Is it not the case that each of us is marginalized (particularly those of us who, because of systemic or other reasons, are made vulnerable and dependent on those with power)? So too in particular are the daughters. It is in this section of the narrative where the universal implications are most noteworthy. The hint of complexity and the historical manner in which both church and academy have viewed Lot's actions toward his daughters have given a somewhat skewed perspective of the daughters. But, we must ask, Who will protect and speak for the vulnerable? What does it mean to be cast into a state of wilderness within one's own home, where decisions are made that point more to death than life? It is exactly in this understanding of the daughters' wilderness that we might most notably identify.

By his own recognition, Lot knows that the men of the city are wicked, and yet his word, "Do to them as you please" (Gen 19:8), strikes such a chord of abandonment: In that moment, all innocence and belonging are eliminated, and the daughters are cast out from inside their family's protection. What we witness additionally outside Lot's protection is more insidious. To the outside world, a child (specifically a daughter in that context) is understood to be under her father's care and protection, and while paternal ownership is ever present, the reality is that the daughters as property—valuable albeit as virgins—are cast away. Lot provides for us a glimpse of terror, of what transpires behind closed doors. It is wilderness behind closed doors.

In Genesis 19:30–37, the more difficult and problematic instance of wilderness takes place in the lives of the daughters of Lot. In these few verses for the most part the various bodies of interpretation have

THE CHALLENGE OF WILDERNESS

dismissed these daughters as immoral and depraved. This is simply one of the sections of the lengthier narrative that is difficult to relate to, empathize with, or justify. Not surprisingly, these daughters are easily dismissed. I would suggest however, that this brief encounter does provide an occasion for an interpretive struggle.

It seems evident to me that this is not an episode that has self-evident universal implications and application. I do believe that there are moments in one's life where particular decisions and choices are made, which, taken out of context, often appear inconceivable, immoral, evil, and (for that matter) ill conceived or contrary to convention. I would propose that at some level we reflect on the daughters' actions in this light. We are led to wonder regarding the depth of their perception about their wilderness experience. It is for the first time in the longer narrative that the daughters (now sisters) speak. As daughters they were voiceless; as sisters they find themselves alone and together, having the capacity to be sisters and to plan. Almost as if to remind us of the convention, the firstborn invites her sister to think of themselves in a most unconventional and devious way. The opening statement of the older sister to the younger is instructive and lends some insight into the thinking and actions of the older sister: "Our father is old" (Gen 19:31). This particular observation is not so much a moment of reflection on a life gone by, but rather reflects the lurking fear that in fact the time has drifted away from Lot to act as father; and his most recent action toward his daughters suggests a painful lack of care for his daughters' fortune. Indeed, given the command by the two visitors to save his family, Lot lingers, and when he finally approaches his sons-in-law, they laugh at him (Gen 19:14). Whatever prospects were present for the daughters at that moment disappeared, and Lot alone relinquished his sense of responsibility over them and respect for them.

As the sisters now face their aged father, who has already sacrificed them to a violent crowd of men, they have come to realize that he is beyond any paternal role, and that they will no longer have a husband in any kind of conventional way. One of the questions generated here does have a universal quality to it. Does one pursue certain things unconventionally, even if they have great potential for pain at all costs? Are the daughters' futures such that they must be pursued at all cost against conventional mores, that they must breach societal norms? Is the price to be paid too costly? Is it possible that the daughters have taken their cue from their father in terms of the level of sacrifice they are willing to make? After all, Lot sacrificed them almost without a second thought (though as costly property) to a group of men that he himself deemed "evil." The narrative spares readers any details or thoughts of the sisters. Only one clear and pronounced reason exists for their actions: to procure a future.

One might very well argue that the sisters did what their father was now incapable of doing, and that in fact he helped with their future without any knowledge. So what might we conclude from this very difficult and troubling episode? Certainly as the daughters find themselves in a wilderness—physically in a cave away from the world (as they believed their situation to be) where they may have husbands—such realities that point to a death of sorts guide them. Their wilderness experience essentially forces them to see the death of their present, and in light of this, to further sacrifice themselves for the sake of their future. Could their actions in any way become normative? I certainly do not think so, and one would be ill-advised to travel that road. However, rather than to dismiss the daughters entirely, it strikes me that we are invited yet again to think of the devastating effects of being in a wilderness where the prospects for life have been extinguished. Another critical issue is not to be missed here. The majority of us who read and study this text cannot identify with the daughters, and two possible conclusions are on account of this. There is perhaps a natural tendency to dismiss the significance either of that with which we cannot identify or of that which we cannot understand. Second, we might in some way wish to evaluate a statement such as this: "I can understand how they feel, but their actions cannot be justified." Of course, the most obvious danger in such a statement is a quest to identify with a given wilderness experience in a way that one cannot. To make such a statement is not to suggest that one cannot form a critical opinion or assessment, but that all of us are a far distance from the daughters. Each of us may (or likely will) have wilderness experiences, and some wilderness experiences may share similarities (perhaps even striking parallels) with the experience of the daughters; but finally, every person has his or her personal, and even unique, wilderness experience.

3

THE CHALLENGE OF WRESTLING WITH GOD AND SELF

THE IDEA OF wrestling with God, or (more broadly put) human/divine wrestling, is not a biblical theme typically elevated to a place of prominence in theological discourse. And when it is, it is often narrowly focused on Genesis 32, well known for the struggle between God or the angel, and Jacob. Yet this theme, generally overlooked in the larger ancestral narratives, presents itself in several instances as a rich theme, filled with complexities and possibilities for understanding our relationship with God. Several branches of Christianity look upon this theme in the same manner that many might view professional wrestling: as wrestling not predisposed to an actual match where the outcome is unknown. But in truth, these narratives suggest that both human and divine participation is such that the possibilities are numerous and broad.

As we begin this chapter, certainly we must pose the question of what it means to wrestle with God. Are the results foregone in favor of the divine, as many believe? Does God not take the human partnership so seriously as to listen to the voice of the human? If indeed these matches are not "fixed," then we must seriously consider the possibility that in some measure, the human will defeat God. For many Christians the very idea sounds preposterous. Yet, I would suggest that the alternative is equally problematic and turns any such encounter into a farce. It seems to me that God does not invite human encounters, struggles of whatever sort, in order for God to flex God's divine muscles. I submit that this very idea is troubling. Does God really need to defeat human beings in order to demonstrate strength and power? I think not. Even though this volume does not explore this theme of power in the human/divine relation in Job, that story stands as a preeminent example of the relentless struggle of the human with the divine. But, of course, it need not always be a matter of such devastating effects and consequences, nor must any such wrestling encounter be only on behalf of oneself and one's family.

In these ancestral episodes, we have superior examples of reasons why wrestling with God is not an isolated issue, or one that is singled out as unique, but one that should take its place as a normal part of life. The phrase "wrestling with God" (like the phrase "wilderness experiences"), while not the most common and well used of biblical metaphors, nonetheless has a critical role in our understanding ourselves, of God, and of our relationship with God. I would suggest that at some level, if we do not struggle or wrestle with God, our faith remains at a very basic level, untested and unexamined. In particular, many of us who have inherited our belief system from relatives are more prone to live a faith that has little place within it for wrestling with God. Yet, it seems that we must struggle or wrestle with God. Even after wrestling for ourselves, we also have to have the faithful courage to wrestle on behalf of others. Abraham sets the stage for understanding one's role in this regard.

WRESTLING FOR THE "OTHER" (GENESIS 18:16–33)

Whereas convention typically brackets this episode of Abraham's pleading to God for the righteous in Sodom and Gomorrah from verses 22–33, it strikes me that beginning at v. 16 we are given an extraordinary insight into a fundamental quality that characterizes the relationship between God and Abraham. There are guideposts along the way in this narrative about the relationship between God and Abraham, and what might be safely established is the fact that the relationship is not one sided.

Abraham has a voice and uses it at certain points, though as we have noticed, he does not at every moment when it might be warranted. Lest this relationship or partnership be misunderstood, it must be pointed out that it is never positioned as an equal relationship. The divine/human relationship cannot be crafted equally. Most of us in the church at some point wonder about our actions in terms of their effect on God. We thus speak of pleasing or displeasing, of sinning or not sinning. It is rare that we hear of God's wondering about a human regarding a specific issue. Here is one of those remarkable instances. In Genesis 18:17–19, we witness a divine soliloquy, wherein God is debating with God's self whether to tell or not to tell Abraham. This instance, as much as any other, emphasizes the notion that there are moments, even to God, when not everything is self-evident.

What we witness here as much as anything is the seriousness with which God takes the relationship with Abraham. Of course, God may do whatever God wishes, for such is the prerogative of the Creator, but here God chooses otherwise and makes nothing short of a radical judgment. God decides that God cannot (and indeed must not) hide what he is about to do. Thus, it is God who introduces the element of trust. If Abraham is to be God's partner to bring about the generations, then at the very outset a foundation of trust must be established, and it is God who challenges himself and makes this determination.

The human partner must know the nature and reasoning behind God's actions. It is precisely this moment in which God reveals God's reasoning that further sets the scene for the wrestling between God and Abraham. This might all seem rather matter-of-fact, but in allowing Abraham into his plans, God demonstrates a particularly serious quality to the partnership. As we read the words in Genesis 18:17–19, we might, in fact, be struck by the notion that in a manner of speaking, God is experiencing an internal wrestling. God takes so seriously the human partnership that God wrestles with himself to determine what the right action might be.

When we are tempted (as often we are) to draw conclusions or to arrive at critical decisions or, most of all, to determine religious or theological truths, this instance of God's internal wrestling should give us pause from quick declarations. It seems to me that here, the issue to focus on is not so much that God reveals plans to Abraham, but that God reveals plans through some kind of internal struggle.

It might have been the right and proper decision to spare no one in Sodom or Gomorrah, for after all the decision is God's; but the issue is that God wrestled before deciding. In Genesis 18:19, we are told that if indeed God expects Abraham and Sarah's household to live by the qualities of justice and righteousness, and with more than a passing implication, then God concludes that God must function by these measures also.

When we have within us deeply ingrained particular ideas about God, it is often not easy (or for that matter desirable) to put these ideas to the test. This is particularly the case if other ideas (or, for the matter, conclusions) are based on the truth of these deeply held beliefs. For many of us who find ourselves in such circumstances, acknowledging divine wrestling is no easy task. Yet, what is the final cost of not doing so? Internal struggle over matters of substance is finally what counts.

In Genesis 19:20, the issue of Sodom and the "outcry" is brought to Abraham's attention. As I read this text, it seems to me that verse 20 is a verse that at the outset must be reckoned with. Given Sodom and Gomorrah's extraordinary history, which some might call "baggage," perhaps we might very well ask, what is the nature of this "outcry"? The good news here is that the Hebrew term ṣeʾaqah is found elsewhere in the Hebrew Bible, and this term is of enormous value (Exod 3:7; Isa 5:7). Certainly, among other things, it informs us about the meaning of the term as it is used elsewhere in the Bible, and (equally important) it informs us of some of the contextual considerations around the word.

While the word "outcry" may or may not be a reference to homosexuality (and it might very well include or not include this issue), we can say with a degree of certainty that the "outcry" in Sodom is not exclusively (or for that matter particularly) about homosexuality. That the text has come down to us with such a narrow and often a nonconstructive focus has hindered the kind of creative and reflective interpretation possible. What we do have is a general description of the gravity of the sin in the city. This is both good and challenging news. The fact that it is general provides some basis for avoiding the pitfall of a narrow, prescriptive idea. The challenge is to determine the "sin" and its gravity, and then to ask and to pursue questions about the implications of the sin.

This text invites us at different moments to wrestle *for* the implications, and then follow by wrestling *with* the implications. Further, wrestling seems quite contrary to what we are expected to be and do as Christians, if indeed we are to follow God. God, as we have witnessed, wrestles, and it is the case that many of us are reluctant to do likewise.

Another significant issue is also at work here. In God's choosing to wrestle with this matter, there is an element of divine vulnerability, for it is entirely the case that what God intended to do would be changed. What we have witnessed in this brief interlude that leads to the divine/human struggle between God and Abraham is the very likely possibility that in wrestling, one might relinquish the "truth" of one's position or change the position or perspective that one holds. We should not imagine that this is a routinely simple endeavor. To take conscious, intentional, personal wrestling that has substantive consequences should not be imagined or construed as anything but difficult.

The theological wrestling between Abraham and God begins in Genesis 18:22. Even though the description declares naturally, perhaps even self-evidently that "Abraham remained standing before the Lord," the subject and object in the sentence are, in fact, reversed in an early textual note. While I am not suggesting that the significance of the struggle is predicated on the note, I would submit that the statement "The Lord stood before Abraham" is remarkable in the fact that in this instance, it is Abraham who is casting a theological argument to God, based on the very principles that God has established for the manner in which humans will function. It seems to me that as brief as this statement is ("Abraham remained standing before the Lord"), it proposes a profound theological question, which indeed must be wrestled with. As daring as the statement is, God is put to the test in something of a vulnerable state, since Abraham in this instance is clearly the one who is posing the questions and, for all practical purposes, is challenging God on the basis of God's own principles. I am not in any way surprised that the textual reference to God standing in front of Abraham is changed for the more acceptable and likely, "Abraham standing before God." Still, a significant *yet* here bodes well for us if it is faced genuinely. Unlike the supposed "fixed" matches of professional wrestling, in this text it seems to me that the unlikely underdog,

Abraham, forces God to consider alternative actions. Not surprising is that many Christians (and perhaps large branches within Christianity) are notably reluctant to view this text from the perspective I am taking. Yet, yet, at what cost!

Abraham begins his theological questioning of God by posing two rhetorically challenging questions, knowing that God could not possibly answer otherwise than expected. Abraham makes his own pronouncement in the form of a question: "Shall not the Judge of all the earth do what is just?" (Gen 18:25b). Based on Abraham's understanding of God, it seems immoral that God would indiscriminately punish the righteous with the wicked. If Abraham's God stands on the very principle that he has established for Abraham and his descendants, then, indeed, God must be challenged. Abraham's question in 18:33 introduces in the biblical canon a profound theological issue that is not only arguably one of the most troubling and pervasive in the Bible; but, indeed, every generation has needed to face the question in some form, namely, theodicy. Every generation has had to struggle with the question of God and evil; of the righteous and the wicked and the manner in which God attends to them in the human sphere. This is a theological issue that must be broached, and God has to reckon with it in the face of the human partner. Yet, this episode is not about who is right, and certainly it is not about Abraham's staking a claim for himself. To be blunt about it, God is unafraid to alert the human partner as to what God's plans are. Moreover, it is clearly not the case that God is making an announcement to Abraham and then moving on. The gravity of the matter is such that Abraham has no choice but to raise moral and theological questions.

As readers, we are left to wonder whether the "outcry" is already specifically known to God, or, as Genesis 18:21 suggests, if God must be personally assured that in fact the "outcry" that has been reported is in fact true, and true to the extent reported. We might, on the basis of this statement ("I must go down and see whether they have done altogether according to the outcry that has come to me.") even begin to conclude that that as of this point there is an element of uncertainty on God's part. Thus, with Abraham's questioning, God must reckon with two major matters: to ascertain the nature and the level of the outcry, and to set the level of punishment to be meted out. If, in fact, the "outcry" is great, then the punishment must be commensurate.

A note that is frequently overlooked is that which is conspicuously absent from the narrative, namely, that there is no indication from God to Abraham about the nature of the punishment. Abraham's question in verse 23 clearly suggests that Abraham knows what God intends to do, or perhaps Abraham too is aware of the greatness of the "outcry." Regardless, Abraham is evidently aware of the manner in which God punishes and, perhaps, of what is on the horizon. In challenging God, Abraham is clearly intimately aware that God must not be indiscriminate and injudicious in his actions. Whereas the narrative leaps from Abraham's being told of the imminent events to Abraham's questioning God, given the gravity of the encounter that is about to ensue, Abraham must have wrestled internally himself. It seems that one does not wantonly approach and challenge God without some sense of oneself.

The very fact that Abraham undertakes this wrestling with God opens for us courage and possibility. As we have noticed, before and after this incident, Abraham is not above reproach, and his humanity is often starkly and painfully evident. Neither the human partnership nor the challenge to God implies that Abraham's humanity and his capacity for error are beyond question. In a way, this is good news for those of us who seek to find meaning in this text and, indeed, seek the assurance and strength of faith to wrestle with God.

In answering Abraham's challenging questions, God is the one who makes clear that an entire city might be saved for a small number of righteous persons. If, in fact, God sees evidence of fifty righteous, then God will forgive the whole city. Thus, it seems that God does not say that the righteous in every circumstance might be punished along with the wicked, but rather God's first pronouncement makes clear that the righteous have the capacity to save the wicked. Moreover, a small number of righteous has the capacity to save a large number of unrighteous. Before all else in this episode, this particular theological idea cannot be cast aside. It would have been easy and perhaps perfectly understandable to let God's answer simply stand as a testimony to God's righteousness. But Abraham does not. In a manner of speaking, Abraham challenges God to the degree that God is willing to forgive. Now, for Abraham, it is not a matter of God's righteousness and justice, but it is a matter of the extent to which God is willing and maybe able to forgive.

What is the ultimate value of being righteous? Abraham could have accepted God's offer of fifty righteous, but instead, in a daring way, pushed the boundaries of what God might accept. There is, I believe, a discernible line between Abraham's daring audacity on the one hand, and not understanding the boundaries of his own humanity, on the other. He acknowledges his finitude, and particularly that in the presence of God, he is nothing but dust and ashes; and yet, this cannot prevent him from posing what he considers to be a question about life and death. In a manner of speaking, Abraham stakes his life for the sake of others. He begins by negotiating for the lives of the unrighteous (Gen 18:23). Abraham's question changes from what he first broached as the central issue (v. 24). Whereas initially Abraham wondered whether God would indeed destroy the righteous with the wicked, when God proposes a solution, God changes the issue, and it is on the basis of this change Abraham proceeds. Abraham would now wrestle with God to determine what it would take to save a city that is evidently overrun with a grave "outcry."

To craft the question in a universal way, somewhat differently, what are the limits of God's grace? Or, are there limits to God's grace and forgiveness? Abraham will discover what the limits and the ends to which God would go to save. Fifty, forty-five, thirty, twenty, ten; Abraham is aware that he is testing his own limits. (He wonders aloud and seeks God's patience and forgiveness for his own audacity [vv. 25–32].) What Abraham discovers, and what we have inherited, is an insight into God's grace. God wrestles with God's plan to destroy and bring about death, even if it is the death of the unrighteous.

What we have as Genesis 18 comes to an end in a moment of disbelief on the part of Abraham. His fear of God's anger as he expresses his view in 18:32 is more a recognition that he cannot finally fathom God's capacity for forgiveness and grace. Whereas he began by challenging God on the basis of God's justice and righteousness, he ends by essentially acknowledging his human limitations, and in an extraordinary moment, it is Abraham who ceases to press God's mercy, and the dialog of questions and answers comes to an end.

Throughout this "wrestling" for the sake of the unrighteous, God's repeated pronouncement of God's latitude of grace and forgiveness is made without any asterisks or footnotes. There is no hedging on the part of God. What is extraordinary here is that Abraham dares to challenge God. We have to be careful here not to immediately conclude that whatever is asked of God will be granted. That kind of simplistic and, I believe, unhelpful theology is not what is at work here.

As I read and reread this text, I return to the issue of "what if." What if Abraham had really "pushed his luck" and had asked God if God would save the city for the sake of one righteous person? What if! This it seems to me is the question that naturally leads one to see the self-evident answer generated through Jesus Christ as the one righteous one who is enough to save all humanity. While from a literary perspective, the Abraham episode should not to be read and understood principally through these christological lenses, in my posing the question about the limits of God's mercy and forgiveness in Jesus Christ, the resounding answer is that it is infinite—costly and infinite. Abraham, like us, finds it perhaps impossible to conceive of divine love, mercy, and forgiveness, which stretches beyond human capacity to imagine.

WRESTLING FOR ONESELF (GENESIS 19)

Genesis 19, as we have already seen in chapter 2 of this book, lends itself to being approached and discussed from a variety of angles. Central to the Genesis 19 narrative is the role of Lot. In particular, the concern in this chapter has to do with Lot's multifaceted wrestling that takes place with the men of Sodom, and later with the angels who try to save him. In my estimation, the very flawed nature of Lot's character manifests itself in a variety of ways in this narrative. As if to set the scene for Lot's struggles with himself and others, Abraham gives Lot the choice to decide which land he would prefer, and it is Sodom that Lot chooses (Gen 13:10–11). On the surface, Lot seems to have chosen well, but in reality as his story develops, the choice of Sodom will prove disastrous for Lot.

Even from this point in the narrative, Lot seeks to define who he is by what is external. We witness in this Genesis 19 episode that Lot seems to have the best intentions, but his actions demonstrate little internal critique or reflection, and consequently with such little thought behind them, Lot's actions prove to be ill conceived and disastrous. While, as readers, we may never know what might have transpired had Lot not "urged strongly" that his visitors stay with him (vv. 2–3), based on the narrative, his actions precipitate a series of devastating events. I would submit that in this episode, Lot's principal struggle is to find himself; it seems that at many points it is painfully apparent that Lot is unsure of who he is.

From the outset, in inviting the two guests to say with him, Lot gives the impression of providing that which is lavish; but in reality, it is a basic, simple meal; in his defense, this is as much a feast as one could have in the midst of such haste (v. 3). Evidently Lot, while attending to the guests within, is unaware of what is happening outside. While he is intent on providing internal hospitality, Lot (it becomes clear) does not "know" the men of the city. Had he known Sodom, it would have likely occurred to him that making an invitation to the visitors would be dangerous. But he "urged them strongly."

It is in Sodom that Lot chose to live and settle his family. Immediately (vv. 4–5), we witness a sense of the dark and evil ways of the men of Sodom. While Lot as an outsider has evidently been welcomed into the city, it is equally clear that foreigners are not welcomed into the city. Lot is unaware of this, and his action to join the men of the city outside further underlines the fact that he is either unaware or reckless. Unlike Abraham, who in Genesis 18 wrestled with himself and God in order to save Sodom, there is at this point no particular discernment on the part of Lot about the evil of the men. Lot does not struggle with whatever internal mechanism he has to guide him in his encounter with the men. Is he so confident in who he is, and in his understanding of and relationship with the men, that he will join them outside with his door closed behind him? He knows of their wickedness and pleads in one sentence, followed by his ill-conceived, devastating offer of his virgin daughters (19:8–9).

It seems that for a long time prior to this moment, Lot might have at least considered his role in the city and his role in his family. It seems that before Lot could understand the men of the city, whom he refers to as "my brothers" (v. 7), he must first have a sense of himself. His present sense of self allows him to substitute one act of violence

for another, or by another. Lot is guided by external indicators and believes that ingratiating himself with the men of the city—and further,
casting out his daughters—is thoughtful and wise. Lot's lack of internal
wrestling causes him to believe that it is preferable to maintain a relationship with the men of the city while destroying the known, genetic,
protective relationship that he has with his daughters. Moreover, Lot's
lack of internal wrestling leaves him unaware of the possibility that in
casting away his daughters to be abused, he will irreparably harm his
relationship with them. One would have thought that even after his
"brothers" of the city turn against him, he would have understood the
consequences of his mistake, but, in fact, Lot's more intense wrestling
was yet to come. Lot has clearly misjudged the city of Sodom, and
while Lot himself never quite understands who he is, it is the men
of the city who starkly remind him that he is an outsider; he is alien
(v. 9). Lot does not belong, and he does not realize that he does not
belong. In his blindness to the fact of his not belonging, he wantonly
severs his daughters' belonging.

It is clearly very easy to be too demanding on Lot. His experience with the men of Sodom, it seems, might at a very minimum, be
enough to generate a serious moment of transformation; but as we
discover, Lot missed the opportunity, and in fact the wrestling that
ensued was intended for the wrong reasons. As if to hint at a parallel
between Lot and the men of the city of Sodom, the narrator notes
that even as Lot *urged* the visitors to come inside, so also the men of
Sodom *pressed hard* on Lot intending to break the door into the house
(vv. 8–9). Lot's lack of internal struggle about his actions and about
the manner in which one must relate in society cast Lot in a position
that makes him more akin to the men outside than to his own kin and
to the men within the house.

The dramatic action of the visitors (v. 10) saved Lot and his
family; they literally and symbolically had to pull Lot from "outside"
and bring him within. Again, in itself this action of rescue might
have been enough to jog his senses about his role toward his family
and about who was righteous and who was wicked, but Lot's lack of
understanding of righteous and wicked will continue to propel him
into difficult and murky waters.

Clearly the visitors (angels) have witnessed more than enough of the "outcry" in Sodom, and without any narrative deliberation, they immediately ask Lot about his family (Gen 19:12). As we have seen in the encounter between Hagar and the angel in the wilderness, the angel poses a question to Hagar, the answer to which seems self-evident: "'Hagar, slave-girl of Sarai, where have you come from and where are you going?'" (Gen 16:8). Yet, as was the case with Hagar, simply soliciting an answer is not what the angels are after. Lot must take ownership, and indeed the struggle for Lot will intensify. Lot will now be placed in a position where urgency matters, and where others cannot navigate the murky waters for him.

The angels have seen to the daughters, and now it is Lot's responsibility to locate the others. The issue here is not that Lot in unaware of the evil, but that he is unable to understand the gravity of the "outcry." Even though he does go to the two prospective sons-in-law and warns them of the impending destruction, he does not seem to have any credibility; they view him as nothing more than a "laughing stock" (Gen 19:14, author's translation). We can never be certain, based on the narrative, of the degree to which Lot took the pronouncement of the angels seriously. The sons-in-law, in laughing at Lot, made their decision not to leave, but it is in Genesis 19:15 that we witness the first evidence of lingering on the part of Lot. Literally and symbolically, Lot will struggle with the angels. He has clearly not fully comprehended the gravity of the situation for himself, and thus his responsibility for others in his household seems to be left in the shadows. As the angels did earlier, they again are the ones who must take the initiative and essentially force Lot into acting.

In Genesis 19:15, two words capture the juxtaposition of the urgency and Lot's hesitation and lingering: "urged" and "seized." Lot is saved together with his family wholly through God's mercy. Despite all that has transpired in Sodom, Lot seems unable to extricate himself. No internal struggle has occurred, and thus whatever external struggles take place, they do so without either an anchor or a compass. It seems to me that one is finally unable to make enlightened and examined decisions about matters of life and death unless one has an internal wrestling match or struggle with the essence that gives shape to the self.

We might think of Socrates's decision to challenge the charges brought against him by the Athenians, made in major part because of his moorings. He had already lived his internal struggles, and thus his decisions were informed. Moreover, even when given the opportunity to be "free" he declined, for this would have run contrary to his ideals and principles. The "examined life" might for our purposes be called the "wrestled life."

Despite the angels' urgent admonition to flee, Lot lingers and negotiates. His decision to wait in the face of the impending disaster demonstrates not only a lack of good judgment, but also by lingering, he endangers the lives of others. Lot ties himself to a place that has shown little goodness, and is shaped by wickedness and death. In wrestling with oneself, particularly in the face of challenges, one will have to at least entertain the distinct possibility of internal and external change. But Lot seems to be so tightly knit to Sodom, to the place and the people, that despite what he has witnessed and lived through, he continues to linger and negotiate. It does take great courage and strength to wrestle with the forces within that bind one to elements of this place, particularly when God has determined that one must loosen the bonds and extricate oneself. Lot finds himself wrestling with the angels—not for insight, blessing, or newness, but rather to negotiate for the best location.

What propels Lot is not the invitation but the fear of death. The irony must not be lost here: Lot is concerned about dying even as he is being pushed to life by the angels. He is certainly motivated by fear of his own death. His focus is on "I" and on "me" in Genesis 19:19–20. If Lot has discerned anything, it is the determination that his life is in danger. If by focusing on the first-person-singular, Lot means to be inclusive, thus far he has shown very little evidence of paternal care. Even with the angels' granting Lot's request that God spare a nearby town, Lot has to be hurried so not to be destroyed with Sodom.

While it is not possible to know what Lot might have been thinking at the time of Sodom's destruction, the city in which to hide and live—and the consequent disconnection from a human community—would lend itself to the daughters' later actions of choosing to become impregnated by their father. Lot's brief argument or struggle with the angels, it seems to me, should not be construed or reduced to

Lot's seeking what is best for him (or for that matter as his persistent trust in the people of Sodom). In not wrestling with his personal set of values or principles, Lot is unable to make reflective or thoughtful distinctions between good and evil or (for that matter) understand a sense of urgency. In failing to have wrestled with himself, but in choosing to wrestle with the angels, who have, in fact, demonstrated the capacity to discern between good and evil, Lot not only paints a remarkably absorbed self-portrait, but I would submit that for a while he endangers the lives of those around him.

Wrestling with oneself, a process wherein honesty and integrity must be at their sharpest point, is absolutely challenging. Certainly there is no indication that wrestling with God is in any way an easy matter, and yet in both of these circumstances (Lot's and Jacob's each wrestling in different ways with angels) it seems to me that the alternative to wrestling with God is more devastating and costly than wrestling with God. In this brief episode, Lot's neglecting to wrestle with the substance of hospitality and sacrifice, to wrestle with belonging and alienation, to wrestle with fear and hope have led to results marked by death.

REFUSING TO LET GO OF GOD (GENESIS 32)

This episode is arguably the most well-known "wrestling match" in the Bible. The very name *Israel* testifies to the significance of the match, and the result is such that it would transform the life and direction of a people. While the wrestling component is one of the most well-known and discussed sections of this chapter of Genesis, the opening section of Genesis 32 is indelibly connected with the wrestling encounter. The centrality of the theophany in this text must, again, like all theophanies, serve as a reminder and assurance that encounters with God do not typically happen to sustain the status quo or to remind us that all is well. Theophanies bring about transformation.

As Genesis 32 opens with the continuing journey of Jacob, angels meet him (Gen 32:1). Many of us have wondered over time what might have been the reason for the sudden appearance of the angels. We might recall that Jacob is undergoing an internal struggle at this point, generated in large part by fear of Esau. The angels seem to appear and are simply there. At least for now there is no particular action. It could be, as Walter Brueggemann has intimated, that the angels serve as protective agents.[1] If this is the case (and I believe that this assertion has substance), then there is both divine and human awareness of the danger that Jacob faces. In this regard, both human and divine messengers are present, and it is clear that only the divine messengers are able to provide protection. Moments arise, we have come to realize, when it is necessary to use messengers to convey either tidings of fear or messages that allay fear, or perhaps both.

Jacob's fear of Esau is palpable—as palpable as Jacob's encounter with Esau in the dark. In sending messengers to Esau, Jacob shows a dimension of intentional deference (Gen 32:13–18). To Esau, Jacob wishes to find favor in his brother's eyes, but one senses that this is the "same old Jacob." Certainly aware of wrestling away his brother's birthright, Jacob knows of the pain and brokenness that he has caused. Jacob's actions beg the question, what might be the most appropriate way to seek forgiveness and reconciliation? Whether this question was on Jacob's mind we do not know, but under the circumstances, it is a question of significant resonance for us. How do we seek forgiveness and reconciliation from the other? One might argue that elements of fear and trepidation will always accompany such a moment. Certainly the one who seeks such forgiveness and reconciliation, as Jacob does, must understand that quest cannot be coerced or hedged for one's personal protection.

Jacob's initial design is to send extensive gifts to his brother. To be sure, there is a place for presents, and the extent of the presents might be taken as indicative of the level of remorse; but in this instance one is not sure of Jacob's conscience. His quest for reconciliation seems to be born out of fear for his life (v. 11). Fear is undoubtedly a part of the journey of reconciliation, but Jacob's fear seems to be singularly self-focused; he is seemingly quite willing to sacrifice others in order to keep his life. Much of what surrounds Jacob's concern has to do with "facing" his brother.

The narrative is held together at points by a number of references to "sight" and "face." Jacob's initial offering to Esau, sent by messengers, has brought back a report about (and perhaps from) Esau that, in fact, Esau wants to see Jacob's face, and this brings fear to Jacob,

---

1. Brueggemann, *Genesis*, 262.

particularly in light of the fact that Esau is accompanied by four hundred men (vv. 6–7). "Face-to-face" interaction must play an essential role in the quest for forgiveness and reconciliation. Forgiveness could not happen from a distance or in the abstract or perhaps (as Jacob might hope) through a messenger.

Jacob assumes (perhaps rightly so) that his brother means to hurt him and to seek vengeance rather than reconciliation, and thus Jacob's level of fear increases. His next plan of action is to "cut his losses" and divide his company (vv. 7–8). Perhaps a less charitable way to view Jacob's decision is to conclude that he is willing to sacrifice half of his company in order to save himself. Perhaps he understands that his brother, Esau, has a legitimate reason for anger, for his vengeful quest.

But whatever wrestling has taken place in Jacob, it seems that his principal concern is self-preservation. Jacob wants to face Esau through the protective veil of his messenger; Esau wants to see Jacob face-to-face. Jacob will have to face this reality. At this point, Jacob knows nothing but fear, and the time for running has ended. Even as his struggle intensifies, Jacob has become increasingly aware of his role.

Unable to manage Esau on his own, Jacob appeals to God—to the God of his ancestors, of those in whose steps he must walk. Jacob's prayer to God is a prayer that acknowledges his shortcomings (v. 10). He has begun the journey of reconciliation, of that which lies within his power to fulfill and of that which can only be fulfilled by God. The beginning of Jacob's trust is most evident in his recalling God's promise: "I will do you good" (v. 9). Jacob will be the bearer and source of God, and given what Jacob has experienced, and perhaps because he has been the source of that which has been "not good," and deceitful against his brother, the contrast is striking. In his crossing the Jordan—something of a symbolic threshold—to usher in an element of newness (cf. Moses and the Red Sea [Exod 14]), Jacob will face both the angel and his brother, Esau, without structure or surrounding force.

There are two particular points of note in Genesis 32:11–12. First, Jacob recognizes that deliverance will not come by his own doing, but deliverance will come only from God. Moreover, while it is Jacob's fear of Esau that seems to consume him, Jacob, unlike Lot, is aware of the pain and death that is likely to come to those around him, including to women and children. To this point, Jacob has not exactly been a picture of a person worthy of being a promise bearer, or of one who has shown particular care and concern for others. Yet, Jacob shows a hint of humanity that bears the mark of one who is worthy.

Second, within a matter of a couple verses, Jacob reiterates even more forcefully God's promise to him. This time, through the use of the infinitive absolute in the Hebrew text, we have the promise expressed as, "I will surely do you good" (v. 12). This is a promise of certainty; and here, with a hint of the Jacob who will not let go of that which he believes to be his, he holds God to God's promise. To be sure, he is concerned about his present predicament, but here in verse 12 he places his present fear of Esau in the larger context of the future, a promise that was made first to Abraham and to his father, Isaac. In praying to God and reminding God of the promises made to him, Jacob is aware that he must face Esau and so proceeds with a plan to do so. He depends on God's deliverance, but deliverance will not come by deputy, and there is no way of reconciling and coming face-to-face with Esau but to do so personally. Even though Jacob's plans include sending servants with presents to meet Esau in the first place, finally it will have to be Jacob who will emerge to face Esau.

Philosopher Emanuel Levinas has argued on the basis of Exodus 33:11 (where we are told that God customarily spoke to Moses face-to-face, as with a friend) that a face-to-face encounter with God brings with it ethical obligations with the human other. Jacob's obligation to Esau is clear, in that he has encountered God face-to-face (Gen 32:30), and now particularly he must encounter his brother face-to-face. In this instance, it is not only a matter of ethical obligations to be fulfilled for Jacob's sake, but also in the manner in which Jacob will proceed with life and relations thereafter.[2] As we read in verse 20, there is still an element of uncertainty in Jacob as to whether he will be accepted, but to move to the future, he must face the present in the person of his brother. Symbolically and literally, darkness and rest will come before meeting Esau. It is in this moment, when Jacob could not have imagined or expected such, that he encounters the divine, and in this encounter he is about to find himself and to be changed forever.

As verse 24 makes clear, Jacob is left alone; with all of his company surrounding him he is left alone to wrestle and finally to find

2. Levinas, *Revelation*, 129–50.

himself. In wrestling, literally one cannot have the structure of company. Moreover it is clear that this was a prolonged struggle, where neither party is willing to surrender, and indeed neither party succumbs to defeat. This is, in general remarkable, and particularly so given that one party is divine. It is God who first seeks to disengage from Jacob, but Jacob would not allow it (v. 26). Even as we hear and read this narrative, there is often a tendency to overlook or sidestep this moment when it is the human being who will not let God go, and not the more common assurance that God will not let us go. Disengagement will not happen until Jacob is satisfied that in fact he will not be left empty handed.

It is not for Jacob to see this divine wrestling adversary face-to-face, as the day breaks. Even as wrestling happens in the dark of the night, blessing comes in the dawning of a new day (vv. 29–31). The transformation of Jacob begins with the changing of his name from *Jacob* to *Israel*. As we witness in many instances within both the Old and the New Testaments, from Abram to Saul, name changing is more than a mere formality; it often signals a dramatic reorientation of one's life. In the case of Jacob, a night of wrestling followed by a morning of blessing will change him forever. In terms of theological implications, at a very basic level, here is an event that places itself in the life sphere of anyone who seeks forgiveness and reconciliation; in whatever way possible or necessary, one must first wrestle with God.

Then we may argue that human forgiveness and reconciliation are driven by and shaped by encountering God in new and dramatic ways. Perhaps encounter occurs in moments like that of Jacob—amidst the fluidity of a dream, when one has little or no control and power. This circumstance (taken both literally and figuratively) underlines the reality that such a wrestling encounter cannot be negotiated or maneuvered to obtain a preset result or conclusion. Jacob understands the significance of receiving a blessing, even as he had tricked his father earlier in the narrative (Gen 27); but now, tellingly, Jacob would not let go of God (Gen 32:26). This remarkable moment must not be glossed over.

We should note that the narrative is not particularly interested in the details of what transpired through the night, except that the struggle lasted through the night. This general sweep of the dream, which sidesteps the details of the actual wrestling, serves an important purpose. Not only is the narrator not interested in these details, but also in not making the details known, the narrator invites the readers and hearers of all generations to inscribe their own details onto the experience of wrestling with God. We enter into Jacob's experience not to hope for a perfect imitation but rather to know the reality of such an encounter with all of its vulnerability and uncertainty.

After Jacob receives the blessing from God (a blessing that, like the wresting match, is not detailed by the narrative), we are reminded that no one wants to journey through life unblessed. The difficult circumstances of Jacob's life and actions are in themselves significant for what they reveal to us. No one is beyond redemption. This particular issue is not to be easily ignored. For a variety of reasons, some of us have come to points in our lives where we imagine that we are beyond redemption; yet from this narrative and from others in the Bible, it is clear that one does not seek redemption when one is whole; rather redemption comes most notably in a state of brokenness—often surrounded by a quality of fear and uncertainty.

Seeing God face-to-face (Gen 32:30) prepares Jacob to confront what at this moment is his greatest fear: seeing his brother face-to-face. He has sought to avoid seeing Esau face-to-face; yet whatever wrestling he will have with Esau that could lead to forgiveness, reconciliation, and redemption cannot be done by "deputies" or messengers, but rather personally, face-to-face. Initiation, sustaining, or restoration of relationships between humans and God can only finally be brokered personally. Moreover, Jacob's personal limping serves as something of a reminder that even as one wrestles with God in a transformative encounter, one is not perfected, but one's finitude continues to be expressed in evident ways. Redemption, restoration, and reconciliation will not likely come without "limping" of some sort. "Limping" should not be construed to mean defeat or loss but rather can be understood as a reminder that such an encounter always brings with it the possibility of some limping. Can one wrestle with God and not expect in some way to be injured? Israel comes into being through pain and struggle, and Israel will limp for the rest of his life with a blessing.

The very name *Israel* is telling and instructive. We are not certain of the etymology of the word *Israel*, though meanings have been ventured such as, "God preserves" or "God protects" or, perhaps, "God struggles." I would suggest that while the etymology of *Israel* is uncertain, nonetheless any of the above definitions would indicate some sense of the significance of the encounter. While Jacob will limp, likely for the rest of his life, he will do so knowing that he is preserved and protected. Jacob's experience at some level strikes a dissonant chord with many Christians who live and work in wealthy or powerful environments, where often it is the case that "blessing" is construed to be God's showering one with material possessions because of one's particular goodness or even righteousness.

Jacob had encountered God in the dark shadows of the night, but the mystery and the hiddenness of the divine, including God's name, will not be revealed. To wrestle with God is not to know fully the mysteries of God. The possible etymological meaning of *Israel* as "God struggles" or "God wrestles" provides an intriguing possibility, in that the name reflects the wrestling of God. Perhaps this is the case, though finally the reality of Jacob's transformation does not change. As Walter Brueggemann insightfully concludes, "The same theology of weakness in power and power in weakness turns the text towards the New Testament and the gospel of the cross."[3] When Jacob finally encounters Esau "face-to-face," he does so with power born out of a weakness.

---

3. Brueggemann, *Genesis,* 271.

4

THE HOPE OF PROMISE

WHILE IT IS possible that promises come with specific timelines and other concrete particularities, more often than not, I believe, promises are made without the often-hoped-for specificities. In the case of Abraham and Sarah, promise is made in the context of uncertainty, powerlessness, and barrenness; and as I have noted earlier, the narrative begins on a note of serious and urgent challenge. Whatever else will transpire in the life of Abraham and Sarah will happen in the seemingly impossible state of barrenness. Until Genesis 11:29, the narrative focus is on the ancestry and posterity of Terah, Abraham's father, and practically nothing is said about Abraham and Sarah's posterity, except the spare and dramatic pronouncement that Sarah is barren.

Even though the scholarly convention is to divide Genesis between *primeval history* and the *ancestral narratives*, the themes of Genesis remind us that such a division, while helpful and important for scholarship, also overlooks significant theological associations between the two sections of Genesis. The theme of *divine promise* is one such theological association that does not allow for the striking separation to which we have become accustomed. The call of Abraham and Sarah, from the very inception, flies in the face of convention; promise for a future will be made in the context of barrenness, and at an age beyond childbearing expectation.

Among the connections between the two sections of Genesis is the topic of new beginnings, regularly generated in the face of nothingness or hopelessness. Whether we understand creation as *creatio ex nihilo* or creation as *order out of chaos*, the promise to Abraham and Sarah, as we witness it in Genesis 11:30, is pronounced in the context of *nothingness*. Moreover, we are invited to notice clearly with Abraham and Sarah that it is precisely the God of all creation who brings into being new communities and the belief that anything is possible. Any- and everything would be possible, and indeed the hope that lies within a divine promise will be generated in time, in God's time.

It is as Brueggemann intimates: the history of Israel does not, in fact, begin *ex nihilo*, nor are the promises made to Abraham and Sarah pronounced in a vacuum.[1] It is precisely this unknown and uncertainty that will cause circumstances to transpire in the lives of Abraham and Sarah that will forever redirect their history and that of their community and their descendants. As we have explored above in chapter 1, hope often dies in the face of barrenness, and yet this is precisely the context in which the promise is pronounced. While it is the case that God makes a promise to Abraham and Sarah, the reality is that the scope of the promise moves beyond their immediate family unit into the uncharted realm of the future.

The divine promises made in Genesis 12:1–4 remind us of at least two things: First, to be sure, humans make promises to one another every moment of our lives. Designed to imagine a changed future, promises by nature cannot be made with an absolute guarantee of fulfillment. Even more so, divine promises are made clearly in a realm where humans are not able to create a particular future. Not surprisingly, the promise to Abraham and Sarah comes into a state of human barrenness, a state of being that human beings by themselves neither can transform nor are capable of changing. God does not simply set out to pronounce promises in challenging circumstances but rather makes promises in human community and circumstances where hope for a future cannot be generated by human ingenuity or creative endeavors.

Hope by its very nature has its core meaning and value in those circumstances when human conditions appear hopeless. Thus, as we reflect on God's promise of hope for Abraham and Sarah, we do so with the acknowledgment that such a future is beyond Abraham and

---

1. Brueggemann, *Genesis,* 116.

Sarah's control. Divine hope is not a substitute for human capability and imagination.

Inasmuch as the spoken word ushered in a new creation in Genesis 1, either *ex nihilo* or through ordering, so also in what appears to be a state of barrenness that brings hopelessness, the spoken word "The Lord said . . ." promises hope. This is no ordinary human hope, certainly not a hope that can be easily fathomed. Indeed, the very assurance lies in the divine promise. The hope of promise as pronounced in Genesis 12:1–4 is not to be construed as enabling human passivity. This is to be an actual hope. Active hope in a divine promise brings with it certain challenges. On the one hand, the faith of the promise-bearer in the one who makes the promise must be such that the impulse to usurp the promise maker's role can never be realized. Both Abraham and Sarah, to varying degrees, succumb to this natural impulse. Thus, an active hope is not designed to allow one to take matters into one's own hands, but to help one to believe in that which cannot be seen, and to hope in a fulfillment in God's time. On the other hand, to wait for God's time is not to relinquish any personal responsibility; active hope unites waiting with expectation, moment to moment, day after day. While Abraham and Sarah will not be able to bring about the fulfillment, they nonetheless actively believe.

An essential ingredient to this hope for the future, this hope of promise, is not to hold on to a present reality that has no future. This inclination is equally tempting, and one must guard against such a vision that does not yield a future of hope. In all of this, the spoken word carries the drama of a future that lies beyond human comprehension. As the creation of the universe was, so also the creation of a people moves beyond the scope of human understanding.

However, the promises made to Abraham and Sarah are not without human responsibility; though the promises are finally not ever a matter of human responsibility. The promises of Genesis 12:1–4 establish a firm relational bonding between God and Abraham, and, through Abraham, between God and all humanity. In pronouncing the promise of descendants and nationhood, God sets out a clear prospect of hope for the future, which is beyond human ingenuity or control. But additional hope for the future is inextricably tied to Abraham, and again through him, all humanity. Whatever the plans that Abraham and Sarah had for their lives, with these promises will come a new and perhaps more intensively hopeful future: one filled with prospects and purpose. Hope will be predicated on a new mandate—on a mandate that cannot be narrowly construed.

The promise cannot be understood in a narrow, parochial, and provincial way, for the very welfare of others will depend on the manner in which Abraham proceeds with his life. One thinks of Jeremiah's painful admonition to the exiles: that their welfare will be tied to that of their captors. Therein will lie their hope (Jeremiah 29). The hope of the future lies not only in Abraham's being blessed but in turn that in his being a blessing to others. Abraham and Sarah's blessings—and those of their descendants—must be connected to the blessing and well-being of all people. The hope for one family's future will be tied to (and indeed will be a generative force for) all peoples. This partnership of hope refuses to embrace distinctions of race and nationality, ethnicity and gender; and, indeed, the treading into the future means that conventional, provincial barricades or glass ceilings will be crushed. While neither Abraham nor Sarah raises objections to this challenging quest, the reality nonetheless is that they will have to renounce whatever it is that holds them in the present.

For many of us who live in a modern society, with all that contemporary society brings, this call of hope for a new future brings a substantial moment of renunciation of ties that bind, and a concurrent willingness to embrace a new vulnerability where the very unknown fluidity of the divine future is all that provides support and sustenance. Here are promises made in ancient times that do not allow us to cling to the present, howsoever secure the present might appear to be. Divine promises are radical assertions in the face of modernity, which lay claim to powers of production and means of newness. This is a genuine difficulty for moderns: to wrap ourselves around the idea of a hope for a future over which we have little or no control.

If there is any qualification made to Abraham, it is that his spoken word and his actions both have the force of shaping the lives of others. The drama of the ending of Genesis 11 and the start of Genesis 12 cannot be missed; one ends on a note of death and a resigned note of the present, while the other ushers in a newness based on a spoken word of promise. In all this, the promise of hope for a future will define faith and the life of faith of those who embrace such a promise. For as often as I read this text, I continue to ponder the nature of hope. As were our ancestors in faith (to whom we look, and who in their pilgrimages have lived lives of hope in the midst of despair, anxiety, hopelessness, and fear), so I am reminded repeatedly that a word that brings hope finds itself most typically resonant in a context where hope is concrete and often rooted in an acknowledgment of human finitude and limitation.

GENESIS 20: HOPE IN THE MIDST OF MISTRUST

It seems that for a while, punctuated by many moments of anxiety, Abraham allows the promise made to him about the future to languish, giving way to what is a human temptation of substance. When it appears that the word of promise disappears from Abraham's vision, he relies on his own ingenuity and wisdom. In fact, Abraham's anxiety not only serves as a clear reminder of human anxiety in the face of a future that can only be shaped by God's word—spoken and fulfilled; but also Abraham's anxiety reminds us that in the face of what might appear to be insurmountable obstacles, we seem to direct our attention and energy naturally in narrowly protective and provincial ways. Yet, as we have discovered from this narrative, not only is the promise beyond human control and constriction, but also, in fact, the promise stretches beyond human pain and distress to the "other"; and rather than hope, the "other" faces devastation: whether or not Abraham intends to bring curse on the "other," the reality is that his actions do bring a curse.

We have witnessed the bringing of a curse elsewhere biblically—for example, in Jonah's action on the ship bound for Tarshish (Jonah 1:3–10). When Jonah thinks only of himself and of his provincial plan, he endangers the life of the innocent. Part of the act of self-preservation brings with it the real possibility of endangering the lives of others, particularly if the one in the position to endanger others has a narrowly construed sense of self.

In Genesis 20, we witness the remarkable juxtaposition of Abraham's lack of faith to Abimelech's striking, perhaps surprising, goodness. This turnabout is clearly not what is expected. Abraham is the one expected to fear God, but it is Abimelech who does; Abraham should be the source of blessing, but instead he brings the possibility of a curse; Abraham should be the one interacting with Yahweh, but instead it is the interaction between God and Abimelech that dominates the narrative landscape. Even as this episode begins with an element of distrust and "otherness" (Abraham himself is an alien), we have a sense the journey to the fulfillment of the promise will continue to face serious challenges based on contingencies. Moreover, even as the hope of the fulfillment proceeds, it seems that Abraham's focus continues to be on the present, while the future remains unimagined. Abraham neglects to understand that the promise is much larger than he is.

Many of the consequences of Abraham's anticipated fear play out in the encounter between Abimelech and Yahweh. As a further reminder, the one who will redefine the present for the sake of the future is God. Moreover, the human vision is set alongside the divine, universal scope. Abimelech, whom Abraham fears, will indeed become a player in the fulfillment, for it is Abimelech's innocence and integrity of heart that are acted upon, and he, the "outsider," is pronounced innocent (Gen 20:6). One is reminded again that God will employ whomever God chooses in the fulfillment of God's promises, including those who are the subject of distrust. The very "other" whom Abraham distrusts is vindicated and deemed pious. Abimelech approaches and questions God in a manner not unlike Abraham's advocacy and questioning of God on behalf of Sodom and Gomorrah in Genesis 18:23. It is God's justice and mercy to which Abimelech appeals, and notably not only for himself but also for his people. One cannot help but witness the contrast between Abimelech and Abraham at this point.

If the hope for the future focuses exclusively on Abraham and his immediate family, as difficult and problematic as it would be, perhaps one could begin to comprehend Abraham's behavior and attitude to the "other." But the covenant moves beyond Abraham into the created order, and this relationship with the other must be established. Abimelech's understanding of his role stands in juxtaposition to Abraham's. It is not about Abimelech alone, as it is not about Abraham alone. Each in his own way represents a larger entity, and each in his own way is evidently willing to sacrifice the future and its prospects for the sake of the present. Yet, in both instances, we are reminded that the future belongs neither to Abraham nor to Abimelech, but to God. We may be tempted to suggest that if both these men were above reproach, then they might have fulfilled the promise. But as is typically the case with God, the future is unfolded *despite*, not *because of*, human choice. The future unfolds in various states of challenges.

One is not impressed by Abraham's reasons for deciding that Abimelech cannot be trusted (Gen 20:11). Perhaps it is the case that the history of the relations might have led Abraham to this conclusion, but such preemptive generalizations are sure to be problematic, as clearly this one is. God will use whomever God desires, including those whom the promise bearer deems unworthy.

Abraham's lack of trust in Abimelech reflects something of his understanding of his faith (and indeed of his trust) in God. Moreover, Abimelech and God have an intense dialog regarding Abimelech's integrity (vv. 4–7). Abimelech pleads his case, and God acknowledges that, indeed, Abimelech is a person of integrity. He is not judged and characterized on the basis of his actions with Sarah; and, in fact, Abraham's concern ("they will kill me because of my wife" [v. 11]) is not even attended to.

Despite this lack of faith on Abraham's part, the fact is that the promise continues for all practical purposes unaltered, as we are again reminded unequivocally that the architect of the promise and its fulfillment is God, and not Abraham. Yet, the promise bearer will also not be abandoned, and as flawed as he might be, he carries the hope for the future, and others will have to give due regard. This preeminence, as Brueggemann suggests, "rests not on Abraham's virtue, but on God's hope."[2]

So, as we read this text with the idea of hope for the future in mind, we are reminded in no uncertain terms that Abraham has been and remains the one set apart for a purpose. From the outset, it has been clear that the journey to fulfillment would not be routine, self-evident, or for that matter without recurring moments of doubt and distrust. This particular episode is in many respects a striking reminder of the challenges of Abraham and the steadfastness of God. The constancy in the narrative is that of God, not of Abraham. It is

2. Ibid., 178.

a challenge to determine the worth of Abraham, except that he is the chosen one; the one who will, in fact, pray for Abimelech, for his restoration. The future, with all its hope, will be realized with the inclusion of all people, for Abraham's distrust of the "other" will only stand in strong distinction to the role of the "other." As if to intensify further the role of God, whereas Abraham brings fear and a curse to Abimelech and his people, God dispels fear and pronounces blessing to the people. The relationship of trust between God and Abimelech further ensures that Abimelech will not be made voiceless, and indeed God empowers the "other" to the degree that Abimelech challenges Abraham. It is the empowered "other" who makes Abraham answer and explain his actions without his inclination to justify them.

HOPE IN THE RIGHT SEASON (GENESIS 21)

The opening verse of Genesis 21 succinctly and unambiguously establishes God as the architect of the promise and its fulfillment. For Sarah, in time, in season, God fulfilled God's promise. This is the essence of the promise and its fulfillment: The time has come, and after the years of wondering, challenge, assurance, and human endeavor, the child of promise is now born. There is nothing about this journey that has been ordinary or routine, and when fulfillment comes, in many respects it occurs in the particularly ordinary circumstance of husband and wife.

But as we know, Abraham and Sarah are not an ordinary couple. This sometimes-neglected aspect of the promise and the birth of Isaac cannot and must not be forgotten. We are reminded in these opening verses that often the mysteries or promises of God occur in the realities of everyday life, in the routine of human circumstances. Miracles, as events far too commonly ascribed to the "otherworldly," indeed also happen in the concreteness of this world. The fulfillment of the promise granted to Sarah recalls for us the fulfillment of the promise made to Hannah: fulfillment in the face of a hopelessness that bore into the very being of Hannah (1 Sam 1–2).

As we reflect on this text as it aids us in characterizing hope deferred, then hope fulfilled for us, I would suggest at least three central ideas to be considered and pursued in understanding the generating theme of *hope in the right season*. First, one of the more overlooked themes in this episode surrounds the centrality of the "spoken word." Even as the "spoken word" dominates the landscape of Genesis 1 and the bringing of creation into being, Genesis 21 also serves as a pointed reminder that the divinely spoken word is the generating principle that brings about the fulfillment of the promise to Abraham and Sarah.

The juxtaposition of *ʾāmar* and *dâbar* in Genesis 21:1 is a seemingly ordinary rendering but in fact serves as a reminder that the creative force bringing about the fulfillment *is* the divine Word. Both these Hebrew terms are grounded in the spoken word. God has given his word; the reputation of God is at stake as God's word is given. As if to underline this and to remind human beings, who are apt to forget, we are told that this is what God had said, and this is what God had promised—literally, this is what God had "worded" to Sarah. Moreover, this all occurred in God's own time. For many, this has been an ongoing challenge. Yet, the spoken word will only be fulfilled in the right season, a season determined by God. But as we have discovered with Abraham and Sarah, the "word" rarely comes as humans expect or in the time frame that humans propose.

As much as any aspect of Genesis 21, "the word of God" has become a casualty of excessive use and misuse. The very quality of the known has also made it into something of a casualty. The "word of God" has to be understood beyond the common religious refrain that has far too often taken on the character of a phrase without concreteness. Indeed the very phrase seems to have found itself with a narrow ownership of certain religious groups. This phrase must move beyond a theological catch phrase that is used as a litmus test for belonging or orthodoxy. Rather, it seems to me that these two variations of the spoken word of God (*ʾāmar* and *dâbar*, *to say* and *to promise*) remind us that the "word of God" is rooted in Scripture, in the very concreteness of events of divine/human encounters. To neglect this history is to neglect that which has been bequeathed to us.

An inherent danger in texts such as these is that their very familiarity poses the possibility (perhaps even probability) of contempt. In general, when Scripture must come to us anew, repeatedly, a moment of newness must not cease to be in our consciousness a moment of astounding wonder. It seems to me that those of us who seek to listen to God's word must at the same time be cognizant of the temptation to make God's word humanity's word in a way that reflects *our* image and *our* timeline. God's word must reflect neither our image nor our timeline. Equally important, as Genesis 21:1 testifies, is ensuring that the divine word is not reduced to that which is abstract and untenable.

Second, even though it is clear that Genesis 21 focuses on the birth of Isaac and the hope for the future that this dramatic birth brings, the fulfillment also brings an unmistakable reminder that it comes in the context of conflict and challenges. Neither the pronouncement nor the fulfillment of a promise will come without pain and difficulty. Indeed, the very journey has been one shaped by a multitude of painful and difficult junctures.

The Hebrew in Genesis 21:9–10 is very instructive in guiding us in our understanding and interpretation of the larger narrative, and in particular toward the ongoing and perplexing reasons behind Sarah's decision to cast away Ishmael and Hagar. Certainly it is easy to conclude that Sarah is jealous, and this would seem to be a natural response for a mother. This idea might more reflect a contemporary sense of who we are and how we understand ourselves, but might not necessarily reflect the guidance of the text. It strikes me that as complex an issue as jealousy is, this section of the text suggests something beyond jealousy.

What exactly was Ishmael doing that caught Sarah's eye, and was this an isolated moment, or (more likely) was this an ongoing issue, so that with the momentous celebration of and for Isaac, Sarah's sharp, emotive maternal instinct came to the fore? I would suggest that Ishmael's action was an ongoing issue, if for no other reason than that we know that Sarah has expressed her emotions similarly before. The convention regarding verse 9 ("But Sarah saw the son of Hagar the Egyptian, whom she had borne to Abraham, playing with her son Isaac.") has been to follow the Greek version, which adds "with her son Isaac." While this certainly has merit and many conclusions have been drawn in this version, nonetheless, it seems to me that the Hebrew rendering has great merit as well. Without the vision of the two brothers playing together, and whatever imagination this might have generated within, Sarah has made a determination on the basis of Ishmael's laughter. Could it be that laughter became the breaking point for Sarah? The very factor that causes the transformation in her life now becomes the point of casting out of Ishmael. Could two sources of laughter not coexist? For Sarah, this coexistence would not be possible. Moreover, it is clear that this is about her son. Her Isaac. Her laughter.

In verse 10, the force and the possible consequences of the act of driving out Ishmael and Hagar must not be underestimated. "Out" in this regard is far away—it is in a way to be excommunicated. The decision has been made to cut them off from the only community they know and from the ones under whose roof they have found protection. Indeed, in casting them away, the years of serving and submitting do not matter. "Out" here means wilderness, and wilderness is inhospitable. Whether or not Sarah has called Ishmael by name is unknown, but we do know that in the instances when there are references, he remains nameless to her, and this particularly in verse 10 strikes a sharp contrast to the manner in which she speaks about Isaac. The concern is "*with my* son," "*with* Isaac." There is precision here, and in this precision, the focus is not only on Isaac, but the focus is exclusively on Isaac.

Even as Isaac is born, Ishmael is in the shadows. The joy of Sarah is matched by the pain of Hagar and Ishmael. Fulfillment will bring for Sarah not only the drama of laughter but also the recognition that this laughter will only continue with displacement. Literally, brothers will not be able to dwell together. Can there be laughter also for Ishmael? Perhaps the years of seeing Ishmael in the house serve as a reminder of what might not have been. Perhaps as long as there had been no "laughter" in the house, Ishmael would be tolerated. But now the time has come, and Ishmael must go. Would his presence dull the laughter? It is Sarah's proclamation that everyone will laugh with her (v. 6), though perhaps not quite everyone. For Sarah everyone who hears will laugh. Will God laugh with Sarah? We know that God hears, and we know that God had heard Hagar and Ishmael, and that God has acted. The only one whose hearing matters had heard the cries of Ishmael and Hagar. Even the sound of the laughter will not silence the voicelessness of the mother and child now about to be exiled.

God had heard before, and with the hearing had brought a promise and blessing to Hagar and Ishmael. Both sons will be granted blessings. The gift of Isaac in God's season has a particular role, but Ishmael is also blessed by God, and he too in God's season will emerge as a free person. Freedom will come out of exile, even as here the advent of laughter brings pain. Despite the manner in which these stories and the respective sons have been reflected upon and characterized over time, the reality is that the sons are not exclusive of each other; and, indeed, their lives will intertwine, and their posterity will forever be connected. Sarah and Abraham must know that wilderness experiences are not beyond the capacity of God, for God hears. Moreover, as *we* hear this story of laughter and the silent despair of Hagar and Ishmael, we are willed to recall that such laughter comes to a couple that once despaired themselves, and that fought to bring fulfillment in *their* time. As Ishmael, the brother who might not know laughter or share in his brother's laughter, moves into the wilderness where there is little prospect for life, he and we might be reminded that God's future of hope and fulfillment is not predicated on the basis of human potential.

Hope springs from the spoken and promising word of God in the midst of conflicts and challenges. Third, hope comes beyond the margin. Even though Sarah seems to cast out Hagar and Ishmael, the reality is that there is no indication that the casting away of Hagar and Ishmael is necessary for the future promise of Isaac. Certainly Sarah's action raises a fundamental question about the mutual coexistence of those who must share a place of belonging. As we witness in God's encounter with Hagar and Ishmael (Gen 21:17–19), God's providence does not end at the margin of human existence. The granting of newness and life moves beyond societal and covenantal constraints to a tapestry that is textured, and at times seemingly messy and remarkably conflicting. But to the infinite, such human boundaries and margins fade into a faraway horizon. Indeed, the celebration of Isaac stands alongside the despair of Ishmael; the feast of Isaac and the famine of Ishmael will all shape the hope of the future.

It seems to me that Sarah's decision (and whatever margins and boundaries we have created to keep others out and apart from those within the circle) flies in the face of God's plan and providence. On whatever basis Sarah's decision might have been made, the text in no way inflicts judgment on Ishmael. Indeed, according to Genesis 21:9, the brothers are playing [Hebrew: "laughing"] together. If the brothers are playing together as the Septuagint and Vulgate establish, or even if only Ishmael is playing/laughing, as the Hebrew suggests, in either scenario the implications for Sarah and for us are striking. The text is clear: it is possible (and circumstances make it necessary) for both the brothers to have laughter. Laughter and joy cannot be reserved only for the "insider." There must be a place for brothers to be together, to know of each other's role, and to be able to laugh together.

In the eyes of God, Ishmael is not discarded. The power granted to Abraham and Sarah is one that God grants, and the freedom that they have been given to make good choices also affords them the opportunity and freedom to make bad and painful ones. This is one such painful choice. There is no inclination that the one elected to carry on the promise will be affected by the "other."

In relief we have here a portrait of a family, a microcosm of a society that makes clear that the coexistence of people with different roles and callings must be realized. If the journey of the promise toward fulfillment is any indication, then certainly one of the lessons learned is that with the fulfillment of hope for a future will also come the distinct possibility of new and ongoing challenges. Hope cannot be construed and shaped only for the ones set apart. We have already witnessed in triplicate the distrust of Abraham (and Isaac) of the Pharaoh, and the consequences that such distrust brought. Accommodation must be given for the "other," for those whose lives are on the margin and beyond.

Sarah does what we are never invited to do: Neither is she, nor are we, invited to choose between the sons. This is not a part of the promise. In casting Ishmael away into the wilderness (a place, paradoxically, of both death and newness to life), Sarah enacts a banishment that hints at death and the end of the journey. But we know that the journey for Hagar and Ishmael was established in the first place by God in the wilderness, running counter to Sarah and Abraham's plans (Gen 16). Even castaways who evidently interfere with plans of the human elect have divine promises granted to them.

The exiling of Hagar and Ishmael again serves a further significant moment in that it not only appeals to readers' hearts, but, in fact, it stands yet again as a moment for divine intervention. Human plans, even the ones instituted by God, cannot, must not, stand as a barricade to the plans of God.

The fulfillment of the promise carried by Isaac will *not* lead to divine abandonment even though there is human rejection. As God once did, so again God will provide for the one who has been cast away from the only community he knows. Genesis 21 might be traditionally bracketed as a text about the birth and laughter of Isaac, but this event does not exhaust divine hope for the "other." For anyone who reads or hears these words, in the midst of the pain comes an unyielding quality of divine hope. All is not lost, though for a while it might appear that way. In planning for Isaac's future, Sarah distresses Ishmael's present and casts his future in doubt. In generations to come, the descendants of Isaac, the sons of Jacob, will encounter the descendants of Ishmael, the Ishmaelites, and it will be an encounter of pain and distrust (Gen 37). The future of these brothers will indeed have far-reaching effects beyond anything that Sarah and Abraham might imagine. But God imagines and provides, and when the final toll is taken on Ishmael, the text makes it clear that Ishmael maintains a present and a future in the midst of despair and of Sarah's abandonment. We know with certainty that as the birth of Isaac comes to fruition, and this divine gift is celebrated—that the rest of creation continues to be blessed.

HOPE IN RECONCILIATION (GENESIS 32–33)

As I have suggested in the previous chapter, fulfillment of a promise comes on the heels of both human and divine encounters. Just as his grandmother Sarah, in her interaction with Hagar and Ishmael, carried a future and hope born of conflict, so also Jacob carried a future and a hope born of conflict—ongoing conflict. Here too in Genesis 32 and 33 we have the peculiar juxtaposition of blessing and conflict held together; and yet on this the future hope will be forged. This episode helps us in creating a perspective for the Isaac and Ishmael relationship. There must be a place in the future where hope for both brothers will come to fruition. The brothers will be reconciled, but reconciliation will not be routinely simple, and indeed it can finally only come about after much angst and fear. This fear and trepidation is further underlined by the divine intervention on their behalf at the eleventh hour, in literally a life-saving drama: Ishmael dying of thirst (Gen 21:19) and Isaac is about to be sacrificed (Gen 22:12).

The intriguing issue in Genesis 32–33 is that Jacob and the future cannot move forward unless both divine and human encounters occur. There is no circumventing the challenge of encounter—a challenge rooted in conflict and fear. But we also know that while there is divine involvement, finally it seems that human conflict and the challenges we face must be resolved in the human sphere. As discussed earlier, Jacob and Esau will, in fact, have to face each other and resolve their dispute before their respective futures will proceed. As we discover in Jacob's journey, he imagines, anticipates, and plans accordingly, as he understands the future to unfold. But, in fact, the future does not unfold as he imagines. He plans to meet his brother, only to first encounter God; and the importance of this juxtaposition cannot be underestimated. Jacob's systematically laid-out plans will be interrupted.

As we have witnessed throughout the Abraham narrative, the journey from promise to fulfillment will include at its very core any number of essential interruptions. The very lives of Abraham and Sarah, of Isaac and Rebekah, of Ishmael and Hagar, and of Esau and Jacob will all be interrupted in ways that they could not have imagined. When lives are interrupted, choices are to be made, and these will often determine the direction of the journey.

For Jacob, this new direction will begin with his insistence on having a blessing. He knows the value of a blessing—a blessing that comes in the midst of fear and distrust. Nothing in this encounter is easy or self-evident; so the encounter mirrors, in a way, the journey to hope and fulfillment. What transpires in the divine encounter is a fundamental change in Jacob. While the divine being remains the divine, it is Jacob who is transformed in the continuation of his journey to fulfillment. Change comes not in the manner one prepares, or (for that matter) one intends but often in a moment of extraordinary surprise. Yet, this change, necessary for the future, is not coercive even though it might very well occur in dark and difficult circumstances.

This theme of "darkness to light" certainly permeates Christian belief and fundamental teachings of the church. Thus we might be reminded that there is no path that allows for a journey from Palm Sunday to Easter without the necessary darkness of the intervening days. Good Friday *does not* simply stand in the way; it *is* the way. When Easter thus arrives, it does so with the scars of Good Friday.

The hope of reconciliation and fulfillment for Jacob will be shaped by scars—scars that become an intrinsic part of his identity. What is significant as darkness turns to light is the fact that Jacob even survives. Jacob wrestles with God, and finally when it is all over, he is not the same, and can never be the same, even as the scar remains. Moreover, Jacob's limp ensures that he will forever be recognized by others; he cannot escape and run; and internally out of weakness will come strength. The future is not determined on the basis of wholeness, strength, or perfection.

So the stage is set for the fraternal reconciliation. While the wrestling is critical and while the transformation is essential, both lead to a climatic fulfillment of hope—hope rooted in a face-to-face encounter. But this face-to-face encounter is part of the idea of hope, and no sooner will Jacob meet Esau than we are left to wonder about Jacob's intention. Is he sincere? We are reminded that reconciliation neither erases the scars of brokenness or deception nor paves a future of hope void of such possibilities. Indeed we witness that despite the open arms with which Esau welcomes Jacob, Jacob nonetheless finds it necessary to deceive his brother. Perhaps, finally, while it is true that Jacob will see Esau face-to-face, even here it is clear that only God will know the heart of Jacob.

It is surely the case that the book of 1 John reflects the core of this narrative in understanding the role of reconciliation between humans and God. Jacob's woundedness is evident, even as he journeys to hope and fulfillment. For the first time in his quest for reconciliation, he does not "hedge" his future. If one could call it "sacrifice," Jacob sacrifices himself for the sake of others for the first time in his journey, and more importantly, Jacob does not sacrifice the future or forge it out of fear and distrust, as he has previously done, and as his father and grandfather before him had.

Facing the "other" as Abraham had discovered, will not come about through disguise, or (for that matter) as Jacob discovered, will come about through a "deputy" or through placing others in front of oneself. What one discovers might very well be surprising, even shocking. Never does it seem to be the case that plans proceed in routine fulfillment. We cast our attention to Luke 15 (Jesus's parable of the two sons), where after making a journey to a faraway place—a place of dread, of despair, and (finally) of self-discovery—the younger son is humbled to imagine that his father could reach out to him in grace and acceptance. Thus he plans accordingly, only thankfully to discover how very wrong he is.

Like this younger son, Jacob does not know what to expect and thus imagines continued estrangement, but instead he is welcomed and embraced by love. But even more so Esau—as the one cast aside, from whom the blessing is stolen, and whose birthright is negotiated away—runs to meet his brother: Esau "fell on his neck and kissed him and they wept" (Gen 33:4). Why Jacob wept we likely will never know: out of shame? Distrust? As one humbled by love? We do not know, but we know that this encounter is anything but what Jacob expected. Like the younger son of Luke 15, Jacob needed to find himself, to know himself as much as one is able to know oneself, before going home. Meeting, facing, embracing, and kissing Esau is indeed coming home for Jacob, even as he had fled for his life.

Clearly the issue of home is not geographical but existential. Before the future unfolds into the unknown, and the promise is fulfilled, Jacob must come home again. Coming home again becomes an essential component of the journey. But in every case of homecoming, the direction will likely differ. Even as Esau welcomes his brother with open arms, he invites Jacob to journey on side by side, together, but Jacob declines. In fact, he in turn invites Esau to journey ahead; who knows the reasons why? Maybe this invitation to journey ahead is a symbolic gesture on the part of Jacob to have Esau; the older is in front.

We know that the journey is far from a destination that is free of turmoil, but for now there is peace between brothers. What we do know from this narrative and from the recounting of the various experiences is that reconciliation, hope, and fulfillment as they occur in human reality will not eventuate in an easy and straightforward manner. Journeys of hope and fulfillment will have at the very least two essential ingredients, namely, divine and human encounters.

Not infrequently we hear and experience within the church an artificially constructed separation between human and divine relationships. While it is true that they are separate, they are, however, certainly not exclusive of each other; and as we have discovered in this narrative, there is an intrinsic connection between human and divine relationships. "The Great Commandment," as Jesus pronounces it, whereby every other commandment stands in its shadow, expresses and accentuates this relationship in its most succinct and sharpest encapsulation: "You shall love the Lord your God with all your heart, and with all your soul, and with all your mind" (Matt 22:37). Moreover, we know biblically that one cannot come to God's altar and assume that all is well with God without both facing the "other," with whom one must reconcile, and even before this, one must look at oneself with the clearest possible vision.

The three episodes explored in this chapter, each in its particular way, magnify the importance of the sometimes-painful journey that must be traveled to hope and fulfillment. In the cases of both Abraham and Jacob (the promise bearers), they seek to circumvent God and to take detours on their journeys; striking is that in both instances, God intervenes in no uncertain way, and they discover that their plans and intensions cannot and indeed must not supersede or circumvent God's. The fact that there are those set apart for a purpose is in no way an indication that the "other" (even when viewed with suspicion) cannot have a role, even a negotiated role to play. In purchasing a plot of land from Shechem's father, Jacob will be inextricably connected with the "other" (Gen 33:19). In naming the altar that he erects *El Elohe Israel* (v. 20), Jacob is at least able to make clear that he now knows the architect of his future and hope.

5

THE HOPE OF BLESSING

As much as any biblical theme, *blessing* finds itself understood and perhaps expressed in a variety of ways in the worldwide Christian community. Certainly the hope of blessing is not predicated on the basis of wealth, land, descendants; the promise of blessing does not depend on a human time frame and is not lodged within a particular political ideology. Blessing, as much as any theme within the Abraham narratives, or, for that matter, in the Bible as a whole, creates resonances of a variety, depending on where we reside or sojourn in the world. Those of us who live in the economically developed parts of the world, where sometimes Christianity is shaped and generated by political ideology and the rhetoric of "earned righteousness," often in these contexts it is more the language of "blessings" rather than "blessing" that is in play. In a world where more is often better, the singular "blessing" preempts the plural "blessings."

It is clear that the fluidity of the open-ended blessing challenges the narrowly construed and very tangible "blessings" that many witness to and hope for in the present. The biblical story reminds us that, finally, to be blessed is not necessarily to have "stuff." One might very well be like Jacob, who is doubly blessed and yet limps fearfully into the future and into the fulfillment of the promise. More likely than not, such is the reality in the world. The ongoing biblical story in both Testaments simply does not allow for an understanding of a blessed life without challenges. Somewhat paradoxically, blessed journeys are traveled on paths that are often difficult and thorny.

As much as any understanding, the recipient of a blessing receives the unfolding of a future beyond what he or she is capable of imagining. A blessing is a pronouncement that says that the last word is lodged neither with humans nor in the reality of the present. And it is finally about the word—the word pronounced by God in the midst of humanity. It is the word that brought creation into being in Genesis 1, and the one spoken to Abraham: "The Lord told him . . . and he went" (Gen 12:1, 4). The gift of blessing refuses to acknowledge or acquiesce to a present that brings to a halt a possibility of tomorrow. Regardless of the personal or communal barricades that we humans create, blessings forge relentlessly into the future. Whatever the conventions under which we find ourselves, it is clear that God will not be contained within or constrained by such conventions. One only need think of Jacob in this regard to have a glimpse of the manner in which divine actions obliterate human conventions, including the privileged place of human righteousness—a place notably constructed by human.

Even though on the surface it might appear that the idea of "blessing" (whether in the divine or human realm) is the same, the reality is that blessing in the human realm and blessing in the divine realm are unavoidably different. Jacob, who, like his great-uncle Laban, is obsessed with wealth, is at the same time seemingly obsessed with blessings. We should not be surprised that in the person of Jacob we see a connection between these two quite strong quests (for blessing and for wealth). The idea of blessing (sharply associated with material possessions) does, however, run against the divine current. Moreover in human convention there is the unmistakable sense that blessing is translated into that which is tangible. There is the further sense in which blessing as defined by human reality is focused on oneself and at some important points seems nontransferable.

BLESSING FOR THE JOURNEY (GENESIS 12)

How do we accommodate disruption to our lives? This is not a fanciful question or one that is without merit or relevance. Indeed, the question presupposes that there will be times in our lives when our lives are disrupted. God is no way interested in playing by human rules—rules that, by definition, do not have the capacity to move beyond human finitude. As the Abraham narrative begins in Genesis 11:30, it does so on the basis of barrenness: the shocking but often realistic human possibility that the future of hope (in terms of progeny) may not happen. In the midst of such reality comes the prospect of hope: not easy or routine hope, but hope that will be grounded in a lengthy journey. But a lengthy journey that begins in barrenness? If we are not immediately shocked by this plan, then we must reflect on this possibility again. How could it be, coupled as the repeated pronouncements of Sarah's barrenness are with the conspicuous mentions of Abraham's advanced years, that we would not be taken aback?

While it is the case that the principal foci of this opening chapter of the Abraham narrative have been the themes of land and progeny, it is clear that the theme of blessing is equally important and woven throughout the fabric of the narrative, and beyond. Like the promises of the land and descendants, both of which pose incredible and immediate challenges, so also we discover challenges with blessing. Blessing holds together the challenge of the future's hope. Abraham is blessed so that he might be a blessing to others, or so that they might bless themselves. The idea of blessing strikes most notably, an eschatological chord, for we see the urgency of "now" in the open-endedness of "then." In many respects both of these words *now* and *then* pose problems for Abraham. This understanding of blessing for Christians should indeed strike a familiar chord even as we live in the tension between "now" and "then." Like blessing, our reality does not exhaust itself in the "now," nor can we, as some are wont to do, seek to plant ourselves firmly in the "then." Neither is acceptable.

The blessing of and to Abraham comes at a moment that immediately establishes two serious challenges: Abraham's age and the dim prospects of a future. Yet, it is precisely these realities that remind us that a blessing cannot and will not be predicated on age or circumstances. One may receive a blessing at any point in one's life. Indeed, the pronouncement of blessing, analogous to the pronouncement of love, is eminently repeatable. And like love, friendship, and freedom, blessing does not come without cost. In fact, all such life-giving and substantive elements that constitute the wholeness of life are costly. We might very well draw an analog for blessing from Dietrich Bonhoeffer's idea of "costly grace." To be sure, grace is free (*unearned*) but never *cheap.* So in the case of Abraham, what does it mean to be granted a blessing? To have a blessed life?

In Genesis 12:1–4, surrounded by promises of land and progeny, Abraham is given a blessing. This is a blessing that comes also in a narrative of displacement of the known for the newness of the unknown. Yes, Abraham is blessed; but now he will live out this blessing even as he seeks to establish a new axis of power and identity? The very community in which he is deeply invested will now give way to a (literal and figurative) place in the future that God will reveal. Indeed, their "place" will not be a place of settledness in any kind of normal sense. For Abraham and Sarah, and for the generations to come, a sense of *place* will have a new meaning. There will need to be an unquantifiable level of trust. Abraham will not be the final architect of his future, but rather, he is reminded, as we are, by the recurring "I": "I will show . . . I will make . . . I will bless" (Gen 12:1–3). Abraham's role is simply to obey, to move as he is called, and to choose carefully the path by which to travel.

The open-endedness of God's future stands in sharp relief against the temptation of the present. The challenge in many respects is also our challenge in the sense that he, like we, will be faced with very real and tempting alternatives. Even as Abraham journeys into the unknown, he will see along the way various established paths on which to travel. Indeed this is exactly one of the aspects of the challenge that we face. If living out a blessing means that we would be protected against all tempting options, and be narrowly guided, then it would not be so much of a challenge. But we do have options, as did Abraham. As we have discovered with other biblical characters who seek to carry on with the journey of promise into the future, the temptation to align oneself with sources of power other than God, such as imperial power (Pharaoh) or established and settled power (the Canaanites) is real and attractive.

Moreover, because the road into the unknown is guided only by God, it is perhaps even understandable why Abraham and others after him may feel inclined to make choices that run counter to God's. I think that it is instructive to reflect briefly on Luke 16:19–31 in this regard (Jesus's parable of the rich man and Lazarus). Then and now, the convention would dictate that the "rich man" in the parable is the one who is blessed, even as blessing is understood as an accumulation of material possessions. Given this understanding of "blessing," what blessing does the poor man have? The reality is that most of us would not align ourselves with Lazarus, and yet it is Lazarus, who, beyond the narrow construct of material possessions in this life, is the one blessed.

Abraham's role, like ours, is not to determine who is deserving or undeserving of a blessing, for indeed all of creation is blessed, and everyone wants to be blessed. One of the factors that must be reckoned with is that a blessing is not to be tightly held for the exclusive needs and benefits of oneself. It is certainly part of the dynamic of blessing that the recipient must be active and not passive. Blessing is not to be so tightly embraced as to be suffocating, but rather, blessing, as we witness in Abraham, is to be lived—lived in the context of the larger world, regardless of whether those around us believe, or subscribe to our ideals. This is one of the challenges of being blessed, a challenge between the trust of what society might deem the "enemy" or "outsider" and what the one who provides providential care dictates. In this way it is very clear that the point of blessing challenges the system of entitlement. No one is entitled and no one is exempt, and thus blessing takes on a more fluid note where equality for the "other" is intentionally established as intrinsic to divine blessing.

Blessing cannot and must not be taken merely as a personal reminder to oneself or a fleeting reminder of God's intention in creation, but rather blessing must be taken as an ongoing reality. The gift of blessing moves from generation to generation. Human equality is thus essential in understanding what it means to be fully human, and given this, blessing, in fact, poses something of a threat to the establishment. This is particularly the case in the promise to Abraham, where it is the divinely spoken word that stands in sharp juxtaposition to the power of human ingenuity. We also know from the very beginning that the promise to Abraham is pronounced in the context of barrenness. There is no more sharper contrast than this: that there is no physical or material evidence and (for that matter) no prospects of such for Abraham to embrace and trust in such a blessing. The state of barrenness by its very definition indicates that in the case of blessing, it would have to be trust. Like land and descendants, the blessing will shape the future.

As blessing comes to fruition in the future, it will cross boundaries and finally establish its meaning most notably in the binding and bonding of all human beings as one. The gift and hope of blessing have an often-neglected social and economic component. It certainly underlines and accentuates God's intention for all of humanity to be equal. In our world, where vying for superiority and power is often for many, the point of departure for measuring the human quest, to be the embodiment of blessing, goes against this current. Moreover, on the basis of both Genesis 12:1–4 and the creation accounts, the very hope of the universe hinges on the ongoing understanding of this fundamental equality. Like the idea of blessing, equality cannot be in theory or in the abstract. Equality borne out of blessing must respect, defend, and nurture the very core of who we are. As much for those of us who might view blessing, as narrowly personal will face a serious challenge. As Abraham discovered, divine blessing does not respect geographical, ethnic, political, or religious boundaries.

Further, how one acts as a bearer of blessing has the potential to bring goodness to others, but conversely one's words or actions might very well create a curse (again as Abraham discovered in his relations with Abimelech). Not only was Abraham not a source of blessing for Abimelech and for the people of Gerar (Gen 20), but also his actions (premeditated ones no less) created a curse, and were it not for God's intervention, there would have been pain, punishment, and suffering for the people of Gerar. Thus, not only is the blessing in vogue when acted upon, but when the bearer of blessing is not engaged for the sake of others, a curse could ensue. Even as Abraham is thinking primarily about himself, he is a source of curses for those he distrusts.

His actions, furthermore, not only affected the present reality of the people, but posed a direct challenge to their future. Even as a promise of progeny and future hope come to Abraham and Sarah in the midst of barrenness, the irony cannot be lost that Abraham's actions bring a state of barrenness on the people of Abimelech's household. We cannot miss the dramatic inversion of potentialities here. The one who bears the blessing also carries the potential to be the source of barrenness and hopelessness for the future. We may wonder whether it was Abimelech who should have paid reparations to Abraham, but while such material reparations are of some significance, it is the possibility of a barren and hopeless future for Abimelech and his people that places in perspective the essence of blessing for Abraham. As this section of the narrative comes to an end (Gen 20), it is instructive for us to note that the narrative concludes foreshadowing a future hope. The present reality will not be the final word. Such is the nature of blessing that, like Abraham, all people will experience what it means to have hope for the future. In the end, blessing compels us to trust God more than we distrust the "other." The trust in God must not be overshadowed by the human capacity to trust the "other." Certainly this is a painful lesson that Abraham learns, and one that must not become a casualty in our time or in any time.

As the Abraham narrative comes to an end in Genesis 23–24, in some respects the story comes full circle, even as it continues in a significant way. While the journey of Abraham and Sarah began with the distinct prospect of death—Sarah is barren and Abraham is old—and thus with no future, the narrative ends with the physical deaths of Sarah and Abraham, but with the promise of a future firmly intact. Inasmuch as Genesis 24 is conspicuous about the seeking of a wife for Isaac, the overall tenor of the chapter is about the future and about Abraham's understanding of the blessing to move into a new generation.

A pervasive quality of blessing runs throughout the section, across a remarkable spectrum: Not only is Abraham blessed, but in addition Rebekah's family grants her a blessing for her journey (Gen 24:60). While the blessing Rebekah receives from her family is an example that is not frequently cited in exploring the theme of blessing, it is, I believe, a significant one. Like Abraham, Rebekah is blessed with the possibility of thousands and ten of thousands of descendants, in addition to the possibility of the conquest and defeat of enemies. Whereas the blessing is granted for Rebekah's immediate journey to Canaan, the blessing also guides her journey into the future, beyond her present. It is, in a way, blessing that grants both descendants and land. This blessing has the extraordinary focus on Rebekah as one who will journey into a future shaped, in the first place, by Abraham. What Rebekah will do, and who she will be on this unknown journey will be to do as Abraham did and to be like Abraham, giving definition for the future.

As we think of this blessing granted to Rebekah, there is a component that strikes a chord for us who journey (literally and, more importantly, figuratively). Without my giving it a second thought in terms of significance, invariably on every occasion when I began a journey, my mother offered a refrain in my early years: "walk good." It was a blessing, a hope of sorts. Perhaps this is one of the implications for contemporary society, namely, that one must have a blessing as one journeys, particularly as one journeys into the unknown. Whether it is a blessing with grand proportions (such as the blessing given to Abraham or Rebekah or Hagar), or a blessing for ordinary journeys to be traveled, blessing is essential. Here too in this particular instance, Rebekah receives a human blessing.

Perhaps we all wait for a divine blessing, but in reality our waiting for a divine blessing must not nullify or cause us to disregard the human blessings that come to us. Even as we journey, we are aware that our encounters along the way will bring potential blessing and goodness to others as well. The blessing to Rebekah will indeed be important as she travels into paths unknown and into conflict and pain. We find this sentiment expressed as clearly in Genesis 15 as in any other text. God's "do not be afraid" (Gen 15:1) is indeed an acknowledgment of divine prescience, and an understanding that for humans, including those who have had divine encounters, the unknown future still poses a substantial challenge. As the journey moves forward, ongoing words of assurance are necessary, indeed, essential.

As Abraham's life comes to an end and as the promise lives on, it is the fact that *he is blessed in all things* (Gen 24:1) that is Abraham's epitaph. Yes, he is blessed; but the blessing, despite the many hurdles, lives on. In Abraham's death, even as his memory lives on, so does the blessing. The entire family is blessed. For the generations to come (who will suffer in bondage in Egypt, who will wander in the wilderness, and who will wonder about the promise and the future), one might be hard pressed to imagine the idea of being blessed. Yet, as much as any idea of blessing, this example resonates with our reality, if not with our ideals. We may be "blessed for the journey," and that is truly a wondrous thing, but we also know from Abraham and his descendants, blessing in itself does not preempt pain and challenges on the journey.

As Abraham's life comes to an end, he seems to understand and know with greater certainty that the promises that he bore must have hope for the future. His very specific instruction and admonition regarding a wife for Isaac testifies at some level to this understanding (Gen 24:3–8). His admonition to his servant points to a marked reversal of his experience. He is intent on not sacrificing the future for the sake of the present, as he had done earlier. The future of hope must be preserved at all costs for the journey to continue.

BLESSING THAT DIVIDES (GENESIS 25:19–34)

As the promise moves from one generation to another, we are reminded that the journey of hope will face renewed challenges. Some of the challenges will seemingly repeat what has transpired earlier. We might very well ask and ponder the question why hope must always be embroiled in conflict and pain; and not only is this the case, but I would suggest that it must be the case. Some things will change (but not the challenges), and specifically in the case of Rebekah, what will change is her state of barrenness. But in this text, there is something additional. Not only does the drama of birth break into the darkness of barrenness, but with it comes a promise that, in many respects, shatters Rebekah's world. This promise of inversion will occur, and it is to Rebekah that the promise is given, without any detail of time and fulfillment. While we reflect on the power of the divinely spoken word as it effected new creation, we have now encountered the role of the humanly spoken word.

In a different way, the human word brings life, even as God hears the human word. As the name *Ishmael* reminds us, God does hear, and in human speech and in God's hearing, life is brought into being—though not necessarily fulfilling human expectations. There is a coming together of both divine and human words, and the result, for Rebekah, creates an extraordinary challenge.

For Rebekah, the gift is also a burden. Certainly one should not typically think of gift as burden; indeed, gifts ought not be viewed as burdensome. But this is no ordinary gift for Rebekah, and this is no ordinary journey that she is a part of. What she physically bears seems burdensome to her, to be sure, even as she wonders aloud to God. Yet, in a more profound way, the divine words that she carries bear both promise and burden. Rebekah's inquiry of God does not suggest that she is interested in a theopolitical answer or discussion; but this is, in fact, what she gets. The very present issue of a pregnancy leads to a pronouncement about the future—a pronouncement that creates conflict and pain. And there is no retreating, for the word has been spoken.

In reading Genesis 25:19–24, and going against the conventional current, we can see clearly that Rebekah is doing precisely what is expected of her, given what God has entrusted to her. According to the custom, and knowing Esau to be the firstborn and thus, by default, the one entitled to the family's birthright, the aged Isaac seeks to pass on the blessing from father to son. Isaac's near blindness certainly leads to the blessing of Jacob. We might suggest that literally Isaac's blindness causes him to err in judgment; but figuratively also, perhaps it is Isaac's blindness that prevents him from understanding the role of Jacob as promise bearer.

Even as Isaac unknowingly does what he must, we realize the unenviable position of Rebekah. The promise told to Rebekah in semisecrecy will not only challenge, but also will undermine social convention; unlike Isaac, Rebekah will act knowingly. Her sacrifice is not for herself, but clearly for the greater good. Indeed, in carrying out her plan of action, she is further aware that in placing Jacob before Esau, she will, in fact, lose both sons. In doing what she does, Rebekah acts contrary to her maternal instincts. Perhaps she is drawn more to Jacob than to Esau, but it is not plausible to imagine that she would casually and thoughtlessly act in a way that would estrange her from her sons and that would sow a seed of danger and feud between her two sons.

Despite some who reduce Rebekah's action to a point of favoritism, favoritism it is not. This idea likely reflects more of what *we* bring to the text than the text itself. Challenging the status quo and the societal convention for the sake of divine promise keeping is anything but favoritism. We cannot and must not overlook the distinct possibility of Rebekah's self-sacrifice. Further, we might argue that like others who have been identified or set apart as promise bearers, Rebekah can in no way, realistically speaking, refuse or decline to bear the promise.

Rebekah's sacrifice might even be understood in part as a model sacrifice. The price for her is dear, and it is clear that she realizes this. She sacrifices what is fiercely maternal. If there is any lingering doubt as to her role, we need only wonder what she has to gain, and the ready answer is, *nothing.*

I would suggest that Rebekah stands as an example of one who has evidently become familiar to readers as a person with distinctly ulterior motives. This kind of familiarity should not generate within us the sort of contempt that refuses to look anew at the text and the circumstances. Rebekah's action is nothing short of radical, in the literal and the most profound sense of the word. What the promise to Rebekah entails, and what Rebekah does, is simply to call into question the manner in which power within society is distributed and executed. Rebekah's action in halting the convention does not so much create a new custom as it gives shape to a new and perfectly legitimate dimension of the status quo. The promise will continue, and, as was the case with Abraham and Sarah, it will continue not as expected or through human design. Thus, those who will recite, openly and boldly, "This is the way it has always been," will have to reckon with new realities, with divine realities that will be neither contained nor constrained by human endeavors.

This promise to Rebekah that two nations are within her (Gen 25:23), inasmuch as it is built on conflict, appears to undermine the central promise of blessing. From the moment that the promise is made to Rebekah, we are reminded that this promise, as it proceeds from generation to generation, will not do so without difficulty and pain. The choices to be made, along with the decision to deceive Isaac and Esau, will come about from those points where there is much to lose. The future will thus not unfold with easy decisions. The pain of cost will be great. We cannot help but believe that Rebekah must have been taken by surprise, as surely this was not what her question of wonderment sought to elicit. Nonetheless, there is no argument or discussion about what God says. Like Hagar, this woman—alone with God—listens and follows, knowing that this promise will not be fulfilled routinely. Also like Hagar, Rebekah is certain to face hardships. Just as Hagar returns to Sarah's household and submits to her, so also Rebekah knows that she will live any curse that comes to Jacob. In this case, by association she will *not* share in his blessing. Hers will be an extended sacrifice.

In the very limited time when she has a moment to speak ("If it is to be this way, why do I live?" [Gen 25:22]), she knows that she too is God's chosen. Hope will come in the midst of challenge and courage. While the text does not indicate that Rebekah was not to discuss the event of God's visiting her, that silence is essentially what happens. Thus, by default she is voiceless. With whom will she speak? How might she explain this visitation of God to Isaac, or, for that matter, to her two sons?

Finally Rebekah's silence is not about scheming, weakness, fear, or favoritism. What Rebekah does goes beyond personal capacity or inclination. It is precisely the *internal conflict* within her that leads her to raise the question of the promise directly with God. We see in Rebekah a person entrusted with divine knowledge, and there is no manner in which she could cast this aside, even for that which is most important to her and for her: that is, good standing with her two sons. For those of us who read or listen to this text and seek to understand it by casting blame on Rebekah, the reality is that the text neither implies nor suggests such a conclusion. God does not in *any* way chastise or blame Rebekah for her actions.

The reality is that this text confounds and affronts us. It challenges our theories of privileges and entitlements, and refuses to bind God's promises by human constraints. Not surprising is that Rebekah is frequently vilified because her actions run counter to societal propriety. In Jacob's becoming the recipient of the blessing, we are forced to understand anew the role of blessing and divine grace. If Jacob does not embody divine grace, then we must rethink what divine grace is all about. He is by any standard undeserving, and, indeed, if it were up to Jacob's deserving capacity, then the blessing and hope for the future would be lodged in another human. But, in fact, we might very well make the point that it does not matter, for finally no one is quite deserving. To be a bearer of blessing is a reflection more of God than of humankind. The manner in which Jacob's life unfolds resembles the way of unfolding life that God promised to his uncle, Ishmael: "He shall be a wild ass of a man, with his hand against everyone, and everyone's hand against him; and he shall live at odds with all his kin" (Gen 16:12).

An additional theme in the Genesis 27 narrative must also be reckoned with and reflected upon. It would be easy to read this narrative and to conclude that at some level human life is fated. We are pressed to understand what the narrative might say about fatalism according to the manner in which contemporary society understands it. Certainly this is a narrative that reminds us and invites us to believe that with God anything is possible. No convention, howsoever prominent and privileged it might be, is beyond divine reach. But what transpires in this narrative is not Epicureanism in whatever manifestation. All of life is not beyond our capacity to be actively involved. In this regard, we are invited to imagine what God destines for us, over and against the sense of epicurean fatalism. In destiny, we are not locked into a place of resignation. Important is that divine destiny allows for human choice. As humans we are, perhaps, destined by God for certain ideals, unfolded in divine time. But, this should not strike us as a future locked and secure. With destiny also comes the possibility of a variety of circumstances that may cause a direction otherwise not taken.

For those in our world who are well established, settled, and comfortable (perhaps imagining that their reality reflects the way things will always be), this narrative announces a sharp cautionary note. For those in our world who see themselves on the outside, who may be poor, oppressed, war torn, and hungry, there is also a sharp cautionary note to resist the temptation to imagine that the present reality is the way life will always be, that life will remain unchanged. Both these realities must imagine—beyond arrogance and resignation—the very distinct possibility that God will act. Our world is filled with both extremes: divided by a sense of, on the one hand, blessed entitlement and, on the other hand, of despair; either end of this spectrum points to an understanding of a restrictive power of God.

THIS AND OTHER WORLDLY BLESSINGS (GENESIS 26)

In this often-overlooked section of the Abraham narrative, placed before us is a portrait of blessing that unfolds in two significant directions. As if to serve as a reminder, Genesis 26 seems to reiterate Abraham's wife/sister episode (Gen 20) but invites us to think differently. Unlike the story in which Abraham, by casting Sarah as his sister, brings the distinct potential of a curse upon Abimelech, this episode has Isaac as a person of peace. As a person of peace, Isaac is not only the bearer of promise, but his presence here points to two significant acts of blessing. While there is no overarching assimilation with Isaac into the community of Abimelech and his people, there is a notable sense in which Isaac becomes peaceably connected with the community of Abimelech and his people.

As the episode ends, Isaac not only maintains his role as a person of peace, but by living in peace with others, he is by default a blessing. As a blessed person, Isaac understands the importance of being a blessing. He embraces those who may be less blessed than he is, or those who, for that matter, have not known what it means to live a blessed life.

One of the important factors to note here is that this narrative invites us to think of blessing outside of quantitative terms. To live in peace with the "other" is a blessing. To share resources (with an understanding that it is not necessary to hoard for oneself at the expense of others) is a peaceful blessing.

A second blessing of hope in this text comes even as' this section of the narrative closes. Our attention is focused on the recurring theme of "digging" in this narrative (Gen 26:18, 19, 21, 25, 32). There will be moments when wells will be filled in (v. 18), but the quest for future hope cannot be cast aside. The hard work of digging for the prospects of water serves as a striking metaphor of hope.

Genesis 26 begins with famine, finds Isaac on the move with some frequency, recounts constant digging of wells, and, meanwhile, notes Isaac's accumulating wealth and, finally, water! This is hope for the future. Whereas once there was "death in famine" (v. 1), now there is "hope in water" (v. 32). But as this text makes clear, there is no easy path here. The journey must be traveled, and at times the traveling will be wearisome, but such is the quest for hope. As Brueggemann suggests, God is the one who provides space for people; it is a necessary ingredient for life and belonging.[1] Belonging and hope for the

---

1. Brueggemann, *Genesis*, 225.

future will finally be based on "space," a place to call home. This, for Abraham, Isaac, and their descendants, will be all the more significant as they continue to be "on the move."

In finding water, there is hope, certainly reminiscent of Hagar's being guided to water (Gen 21:19), a reference that is indelibly connected to the promise of descendants for the future. Perhaps as much as anything, a future without the prospects of water or land is a future without hope. Indeed, to have a blessed life, one must have the very fundamental essentials: a sense of place, a sense of belonging, and water as a gift of life.

Thus far, for the most part, we have examined the biblical presence of divine blessing and its implications for the promise bearers then, and for those who live in hope now. It seems to me that the presence of divine blessing remains central. Yet, Genesis 26 invites us to reflect in additional ways on the manner in which blessing, hope, and existential realities might come together. Here we have a resounding call to be attentive to the needs and hopes that matter in the world in which we find ourselves. Blessing brings hope for a future, but it also brings concreteness in the present.

It seems to me that this text casts a nonnegotiable understanding on the dialectical nature of blessing, though there is no indication that this particular moment in the text can be translated in a universal way that fits every scenario. Indeed, we know that not everyone who is blessed will necessarily have material possessions. And we must be careful not to quantify blessing in this way; for even biblically there is no universal quantifying guide. As I have suggested earlier in this study, we cannot assume in superficial ways that blessing might be equated with possessions. Thus for all who read and hear the words of this text, there is a cautionary note: do not imagine our reality (whatever it might be) to be the definitive understanding of what it means to be blessed universally. Particularly as we think of the ways that some societies and nations explain and justify oppression of others, we are cautioned about such interpretation and appropriation of the biblical text.

While it is true that as Christians we do not imagine this life as the "final word," we must not employ the biblical text as a means of oppression, while inviting the oppressed to believe in the blessing of

the "other world." At the very least, this is a corrupt way to use the
Bible, and certainly it is destructive. To borrow a phrase from Samuel
Terrien, this would be nothing short of "abusive exegesis."[2] So how
do we then approach these undeniable expressions of blessings in
this chapter?

Blessings, even those expressed by human characters in the Bible,
come as gifts from God. But as we have discovered also, quite persis-
tently, there is no timeline for blessing, and it is likely to be the case
that whatever the established human expectations are, they are not
likely to be met according to a timeline. The testimony that we witness
in this chapter establishes clearly that, indeed, blessings are possible in
our present realities. As much as any narrative, the Abraham narrative
makes clear that no one is entitled or equipped to determine whether
or when the promise of blessing will be fulfilled.

For all of us who wonder about the immediate moments and
events that surround us, this section of the narrative is in itself a blessing. No one is empowered to deny another the possibility of living
this life with the potential for material blessings. What is striking in
this text is the clarity that suggests that no conflict between the divine
and that which we might think of as prosperity. Genesis 27 further
underlines the possibility of a peaceful existence between divine blessing and material prosperity. It seems impossible that we can speak of
peace if one constantly has to be on the move to find security and
belonging and fundamental sources of sustenance.

The texts aid in defining need and abundance. What constitutes
abundance? One of the challenges that many of us in the "developed
world" face in this regard is a definition of prosperity and abundance
that reflects our level of necessity and need. But our definition of prosperity need not be (indeed must not be) determined by our necessity.
Blessings for the present and future must not be equated or confused
with excess. Basic necessity is a blessing that is the foundation of all
peace and belonging. In a world where there is abundance, where there
is the possibility for much, and certainly enough for all, everyone must
have a chance to share in this blessing.

---

2. Terrien, *Till the Heart Sings*, 126.

LONGING FOR A BLESSING (GENESIS 27)

This text hearkens back to Genesis 25 and the issuance of the promise. This section of the larger narrative is fraught with conflict, a continuing, deeply embedded theme of challenge and difficulty. Genesis 27 serves as a further reminder that howsoever important or significant a blessing or promise might be, the reality remains that one is not likely to be exempt, to imagine, or to expect to be exempt from conflict or challenge. We have witnessed throughout these narratives ongoing tension between the vertical and horizontal relationships that must be maintained in proper respect, but often are not. The life of the promise first made to Abraham, and that moves to fulfillment through Isaac and Jacob, will clearly not be accomplished through the horizontal machinations of humans.

Many within the church, particularly those who reside in economically and technologically advanced societies, find such an idea particularly challenging. Where human capacity is such that one comes to believe that anything is humanly possible, the idea of a proper tension between the horizontal and the vertical is even more pronounced. The reality is that the vertical cannot in any way be sidelined or erased from the equation. God's role is non-negotiable. As if to underline this theme, the narrative presents quests (which we have witnessed) by Abraham and Sarah, by Isaac, and by Jacob to fulfill the promise by themselves—and at various levels disregarding the essential and irreplaceable vertical component.

From time to time, humans have sought to shape or control nature—from redirecting rivers to building dams. While these quests are often not without merit, the possibility exists that human ingenuity and power might very well for a while seem to work; but there are also ultimate issues that frequently bring about challenges. Divine blessing cannot be harnessed and narrowly redirected to fit human needs and interests. Divine blessing will, indeed, have its own way and direction, and often this will come to the shock and dismay of the human participants.

Blessing is not without price and cost. Part of this cost involves the very sacrifice of self. Regardless of the identity of the participant, there cannot be human ownership of divine blessing. To relinquish such a hold and to allow God to open a future for us is no mean challenge. Yet, as we reflect on the implications of these narratives, it seems clear to me that there is no alternative, but to relinquish any singular hold we might seek to have on the unfolding of the future and the fulfillment of blessing. One of the more insidious ways of such ownership might be in the form of such intense preoccupation with the blessing that, in fact, preoccupation with the blessing could become more of a burden than it needs to be.

In understanding the dialectical relationship between the vertical and the horizontal idiom, we must resist the temptation to choose one or the other. And this is a serious temptation. In fact, this temptation to grant exclusivity to human power and ingenuity to achieve and fulfill is great and very inviting. As we have observed before in these Abraham narratives, there is no mistaking the human quest and the invariable price that this quest brings. Yet, the temptation we face is not only to human exclusivity, but also to the exclusive focus on either human or divine power. The reality is that focusing exclusively on either direction poses significant challenges for contemporary society. On the one hand, the horizontal trajectory is quite tempting in that human beings, with all of the various developments in the world, not surprisingly may believe that we have the capacity to bring about any reality we choose. But the fulfillment of blessing is more than the engagement of the truism that if one puts one's mind to something, then anything is possible. Thus the more pronounced the human intellectual and developmental capacity is, the more tempting it is to reduce the vertical component.

On the other hand, equally important is the propensity for some Christians to "wait" on divine intervention and in so doing to effectively relinquish human responsibility. This tendency is in some respects somewhat more insidious and dangerous than the tendency to overplay human possibility. Often this perspective is couched in religious or theological vocabulary. Thus, some of us may be left to wonder how it is that we could question the pronouncement that the fulfillment of divine promises is the sole prerogative of God.

Invariably this kind of statement is likely to bring either silent affirmation or acquiescence. But, in fact, neither of these should be an appropriate option. In the face of social ills, systemic injustices, inequities, systemic terror, or other evils, it is arguably morally reprehensible to apply "in God's time" as the patent answer. We might in this regard recall Martin Luther King's wisdom that in the face of injustice, "waiting" means "never"; for, ultimately, "time" is neutral.[3] In the context of injustice, this perspective, so very suggestive of faithfulness in divine time, is, in fact, a recasting of human power. It is the horizontal decision of what the vertical might do.

The posture of waiting is a less-than-subtle usurpation of divine power in order to maintain the status quo when the status quo suits one's position in life. Simply to say that the evils or ills in society will be rectified, transformed, or cleansed entirely in God's time is a serious relinquishing of human responsibility and care for one another. To be one's keeper is not to be determined exclusively on the basis of God's initiative. In some notable instances, such a perspective or response might with justification be construed as maintaining injustices for one's personal investment. Such positioning, if generated from a position of power (as often is the case), undermines the horizontal role and, in fact, in so doing paradoxically seeks to limit God. The point here is that an ongoing proper tension between the vertical and the horizontal is essential to living out the blessing for the future.

Blessing brings an undeniable and an unmistakable claim that the future of the blessed life cannot and, more importantly, must not remain the same as the present. Moreover, as we have seen, the transformation of life will not be isolated and connected only with the individual. Particularly in the case of Jacob, the implications of transformation do begin with Jacob, but the circle of transformation widens quickly and inseparably to brothers, to parents, to community, and then to the nation. What is clear to us is that blessing cannot and will not be contained in narrow confines.

Genesis 27 redefines and sharpens the question, "am I my brother's keeper?" Not only is the immediate rhetorical answer yes, but the insistent recurring yes moves from one generation into another. Each of us is invested in the life and destiny of the other. One of the ongoing challenges that this text poses for some Christians who live in economically developed nations is the emphasis that calls us away from narrowly focusing on the individual. As Brueggemann

3. Martin Luther King Jr., *Letter from Birmingham Jail*.

points out, there is a "massive and unqualified" quality to blessing.[4] The blessing might be granted to the individual, but it is never only for the individual. As Genesis 27:28 makes clear, the entire earth is the field in which the blessing is to be played out.

Specifically in Genesis 27:29, matters of politics and history are also addressed. If this text makes anything clear, it is the fact that the individual and the interests and quests therein are significant and important only insofar as these are understood in light of communal interests. However we define "community," the text makes certain that all societies and nations, communities and families may not promote individual needs and interests at the expense of the community. For many of us, this is a genuine challenge and thus in itself is remarkably potent.

We have encountered before in a number of biblical texts power in the spoken word. It would be simple to cast this singularly as a biblical phenomenon that retains its importance only as a historical matter. However, it seems evident to me that as with other themes, there are implications for contemporary society. Certainly we live in a world where particular words of the powerful are frequently misconstrued and often viewed with a quality of cynicism. The biblical text reminds us that this need not be the case. Words, and particularly words of promise, should not be used casually, or simply to serve one's narrow purposes. That is to say, words are to be more than tools; words are to be used for more than to avoid challenging, difficult, or transformative issues. Biblical words have power, and such words or variations cannot be employed only for one's personal purposes. Yet, the biblical words are more than cautionary words. We are not invited simply to be careful, but to understand the force of our words and the various possibilities. Certainly it would be far too easy to conclude that only divine words have power to transform. We have evidence from countless instances of human words having been pronounced as both blessing and curse. Moreover, while we might be invited to be attentive to our vocabulary and to our mode of speech, this is more than a call to employ clever technicalities or the use of semantics.

Additionally, the text of the Abraham narratives invites us to understand the role of power in our lives and in our surrounding world.

---

4. Brueggemann, *Genesis,* 232.

As we have witnessed repeatedly in biblical texts, there are varieties of power, and in this regard we are not allowed to collapse "power" into a singular category with narrow reference points. What does it mean to have power? This question as much as any other dispels any narrow definition of power alignment. The tendency to ascribe primacy to military or physical force, or to economic or material matters is quickly dispelled. The Abraham narrative indeed makes clear that the biblical understanding of power defies any conventional understanding constrained by Western norms. Perhaps we are well advised to cast our vision onto the role of power in the New Testament, where Jesus is brought forth in a state of what many would call powerlessness, and at the end of his life he defined power through the act of washing the feet of those around him. To be blessed, therefore, is beyond the conventional categorization of having power, and it is certainly beyond the notion of luck. Indeed, some believe that lottery winners are blessed; but winning the lottery is luck—maybe luck of great magnitude—but luck nonetheless.

As if to underline the incongruity between power (as blessing) and the more conventional understanding of power (as force), the narrative motivates Jacob by fear; Jacob believes that he is incapable of defeating his brother militarily. Jacob, like many of us, is yet unaware of what it means to have power through being blessed. Indeed, we have witnessed repeatedly in the Bible that power is not to be construed as or through force. Faith in the unfolding of a future is power, and serves as a substantive challenge to the typical understanding of power as physical force.

Living a blessed life is more than a truism or a fad on a bumper sticker. Time and again, we have been reminded that there is nothing ordinary or routine about living a blessed life. Anyone who imagines that the blessed life is straightforward is missing an essential biblical component. That it is *not* straightforward is a reminder that the direction of the blessed life is beyond human control. The text reminds us in that those of us who are inclined to proceed with certitude in our determinations about the future are prevented through divine preemption from such a positioning. The only certainty about a blessed life is the knowledge that one is blessed, but how that journey is traveled one cannot be sure.

In the episodes examined here, we are compelled to abandon our understanding and knowledge of who the blessed are. The ways of God are so inscrutable that God will choose whomever God so chooses, and the life of the blessed will be played out in whatever pattern God so determines. In a real way, we human beings must understand and come to accept this reality—that finally it is not for human beings to discover or elicit all of the answers to the divine promises and initiatives. This is a particular challenge to some sections of Christendom, in large part because it strikes an antithetical chord to the current insatiable quest for answers to life's questions. Indeed, this invitation to live with the openness of promise stands in sharp contrast to human belief that humans have the infinite capacity to discern all things.

6

THE HOPE OF FULFILLMENT

IN SPEAKING OF fulfillment we must be pointedly careful so as not to pit the Old Testament against the New Testament. One of the important aspects of this final chapter is to develop the following idea: Not only do *promise* and *fulfillment* occur within the Old Testament and therefore are not dependent on the New Testament, but also *promise* and *fulfillment* occur within particular narratives. But even as this chapter brings to an end this study, it is the hope of fulfillment that is at stake. This chapter will focus largely on Genesis 22, commonly referred to in Christian circles as the "Sacrifice of Isaac." Even though the Abraham narrative continues after Genesis 22, in many respects Genesis 22, with its unparalleled theological difficulty and challenge, brings a denouement to the study. One of the connective themes between the creation accounts, the Abraham narratives, and the Exodus event is that of beginnings: the creation of the universe, the establishment of a family with future prospects, and the defining of nationhood, with all that that implies. But as we have witnessed in each case, these are stories that are more than cosmogonies and beginnings.

When we first encountered Abraham and Sarah in Genesis 12, we knew that it would be a long journey home. This would be but the first step in a very long journey, and we had no idea what this journey home would entail. We had no idea about the nature of the journey, the obstacles, and the hurdles of sheer terror. We could not have imagined. Given this focus, we might readily wonder how we might presume any hope of fulfillment when the very prospect of hope appears to die. Yet, I would propose that Genesis 22 is precisely the text that must be explored. There is no way around facing the important question that a test such as this generates. How does God, or how might God, test us today wherever we might find ourselves? This seems to me to be both a pertinent and important question to pursue, particularly if we hold divine testing as an integral part of our belief system.

For the most part, if a system of belief includes a notion of divine testing, then such a notion of testing cannot be general, and rather disconnected from the concreteness of everyday life. Yet, such a general notion of divine testing seems to be repeated rather routinely in petitions such as "do not put us to the test." If it is to be part of our belief, then testing has to be reckoned with concretely as much as possible.

Moreover, not only the issue of testing is important, but also the manner in which we respond to testing is important. The idea here is no more for us to create a prescriptive category of tests than to imagine that the various "tests" of the Bible compose an exhaustive list. One has to prepare to be tested in whatever way God chooses, and in whatever environment in which one finds oneself.

As we reflect on the story and the various themes, we cannot reduce it to a mere historical reminiscence. Rather, we are invited to pursue and ponder questions that have strong implications and are relentless. So in what way might God test? Because we no longer encounter God in "burning bushes" or "pillars of cloud" does not or should not suggest that encounters or tests have disappeared. Because we are not likely to be asked by God to sacrifice our child should not in any way be construed as an indication that we will not face challenging tests. Moreover, we should contemplate in real and concrete ways what occurs in our everyday lives, and not seek either to exempt ourselves or to create scenarios of abstract testing.

As in the case of the sacrifice of Isaac, the concreteness might very well revolve around matters of life and death. One of the serious realities of testing is that it has the potential to put our very faith under fire. Divine testing places that which is central in our lives under the most serious of challenges. The questions that quickly emerge in such a scenario form the centerpiece of our lives: How tightly will we hold on to that which we have deemed precious and central? What is it that demands our singular focus and attention? Is it possible that what demands our attention might very well be at serious variance with the loyalty and faith we testify to God?

In some respects, Genesis 22 represents very well the proverb "Familiarity breeds contempt." The good news is that Genesis 22 is a well-known text; indeed, for many of us who are familiar with this extraordinary story, conclusions about meaning and implications have already been drawn. For many Christians, this story has one universal meaning, namely the unwavering faith of Abraham. But this kind of familiar conclusion also brings with it certain problems. To be clear here, to question such a common conclusion is in no way to suggest that the faith and faithfulness of Abraham are not legitimate themes of the story, but rather only to note that these themes are not exhaustive because of the expanse of meaning within the text.

When we first encounter Abraham and Sarah, as the narrative begins in Genesis 12 with the call of Abraham (an extraordinary test in its own way), faith in the hope of a future leads them on a journey into the unknown. So also Genesis 22 imagines a reality where serious life-giving and future-shaping decisions have to be made. Nowhere else but in this narrative is such a dramatic choice to be made. If there is ever a circumstance in the Bible where the human being is given a moment to make a serious choice, this is surely such an instance.

Even though there is a sense of straightforwardness in God's command to sacrifice, it is clear, on a careful reading, that by necessity a multitude of questions must be answered. Abraham, it is evident, must not only face the reality of an extraordinary father-son moment (for the second time under different circumstances), but also in the midst of the drama, we know that he is no longer Abram but is now Abraham; his story cannot be narrowly defined as pertaining only to his progeny and future; for it now will pertain to multitudes, for generations to come. So we consider questions such as, Will Abraham be able to endure the test? Will God be able to endure the test? This sacrifice of Isaac is as much a test for God as it is for Abraham.

In this well-known scenario, the one who stands to gain or lose seems to be Abraham, though I would suggest that the vulnerability of God (an idea not frequently explored) is also quite evident. Yet, as we have witnessed before, and here again, Abraham does have legitimate power to make choices. Terence Fretheim suggests that "God initiates the test to gain divine certainty. . . . Testing must be understood relationally, not legalistically. Life in relationship inevitably brings tests of loyalty . . . . The test is as real for God as it is for Abraham."[1] We might even boldly suggest that God has much to lose here. We must believe that God understands the magnitude of the test.

As we arrive at this juncture in the narrative, particularly as this story follows the drama of Genesis 21 and the long-awaited birth of Isaac, any careful reader would immediately be shocked by the unexpected circumstances and developments. Few of us are able to read this story and not wonder silently or aloud if this journey to the fulfillment of God's promise to Abraham (Gen 12:1–4), after all this time and after all the angst, has been for naught. Will not the prospects of Isaac's death bring Abraham and Sarah again into a state of barrenness, similar to their state in Genesis 12, except in this instance with substantially more pain, even as their future disappears? Far too much is riding on this moment for it to be recast using empty religious rhetoric and vocabulary.

As if a textual reminder that we cannot possibly know the future, this test of Abraham comes unannounced. The reality is that we could not have seen this event coming. There is no indication in the body of the story up to this point that hints that such a test could be possible, yet in what is already an extraordinary story comes this truly extraordinary development. We could not have been less prepared. But herein lies a fundamental direction in this broader Abraham narrative. It is finally about hope; hope in the face of such utter hopelessness and barrenness that nothing but unimaginable faith in a future over which there is no human control will maintain hope. So, then, why should we be surprised? Yet, we are, and we should be surprised. None of this is clear.

In truth I am utterly shocked by Genesis 22—repeatedly shocked. I have finally persuaded myself that this story should be perpetually shocking. Given all that has transpired in the journey of Abraham and Sarah thus far, how could God make such a demand! But God does, and once again we are reminded that the future is not controlled by humans. If, in reading the Abraham narrative, we have wondered

---

1. Fretheim, "Genesis," 53–54.

about the necessity of faith for the journey right from the beginning (and I cannot imagine why there should be any such question), then any such wondering is dispelled with Genesis 22. This is a story that affirms or ends the journey. There is no "in-between" or "sort-of" response to this text.

The text begins with the seemingly innocuous words, "After these things God tested Abraham," leading us to believe that this is the first time that Abraham is being tested. But since we know otherwise, we begin to wonder what is at stake—clearly for Abraham and certainly for God. If this is truly a test, does it not make God vulnerable with the gravity of the choice given to Abraham?

Indeed, much is at stake here. It is in this text that we encounter Abraham being represented at the crossroads between the vertical and the horizontal, between the demands of heaven and the responsibilities of earth. Is this tension to be lived, and can both demands and responsibilities be satisfied? Remarkably, Abraham responds to the beckoning of both heaven (God) and earth (Isaac) with the same response, "Here I am!" So what might we say about Abraham's response to God? On the one hand, without our attending to the consequential aspects of his response, certainly Abraham's responding as he does is a model of faith and faithfulness.

The immediacy of faithful believing, not knowing where the future leads or ends, is a mark of distinction. So we ask, is this prompt and immediate response enough? Is this the best and most appropriate expression of faith? Certainly as we read this text and hear these words, our attention wanders to Jesus's call of the disciples—the call to disciples in a variety of places and circumstances; disciples leaving various positions, roles, stations in life. What they share with Abraham is the consistent immediacy of their responses. In every instance, we are able to understand why we would question, reason, challenge, negotiate—but none of these hesitations is present for Abraham or for the disciples. We note also that the immediate answers are not to be construed as casual. Like Abraham, the disciples stand to suffer loss of family, friends, and all sorts of security. But their answer is clear and unequivocal.

To what does Abraham say yes? At one level, it does strike one as a question that merits asking even as the answer seems self-evident.

Yet, is Abraham's yes only a response to the command to sacrifice his son, or is it also a yes to God's provision? It seems to me that the text invites us to focus not narrowly on the command to sacrifice but on the history of the relationship between God and Abraham. Moreover, the text invites us to think of the "test" as including both sacrifice and provision.

As we witnessed in Genesis 12, Abraham's faithfulness is at some level sharpened by the immediate and unequivocal nature of his response. By lauding Abraham's quick answer to God, I do not wish in any way to imply or suggest that "waiting" is to be equated with a lack of faith; but there is a marked distinction in a response that is immediate and without internal negotiation. In the verses of the narrative, as we have seen elsewhere, the intent of the narrator is not to spell out every detail or fill every gap in the actual sacrifice. Much, perhaps far too much for many of us, is left unsaid. The idea, further, is not to embellish the narrative with much discourse, let alone with excessive discourse between Abraham and God or between Abraham and Isaac. We read along, journey along, in our own stunned silence, with all the wonderings that we generate along the way. Statements are made, questions arise, and we are left to draw a variety of conclusions.

In any number of biblical texts, resolutions do not come along readily (e.g., the manner in which Jonah ends), and here too we are left to draw our own conclusions. In clearly significant ways, this story offers a profound invitation to question. Here too is one of the many challenges of the proverb "familiarity breeds contempt," for it is the case that many Christians familiar with the text are not open to the possibility that there will always be new elements and components to the story. The story might appear static (though it certainly is not); and who we are when we come to the story is ever changing. We must have the courage to acknowledge that in the raising of theological and social questions, the textual waters may be muddied, but there will certainly be integrity in our personal engagement.

There is also the unmistakable difference in perspective between the circumstances surrounding Genesis 12 and Genesis 22. The former has all the prospects of life and potential, and the possibility of a future unimagined; in the latter, the consequences certainly appear dire: the distinct possibility exists for the death of a future. The drama could not be more intensely outlined.

It is immediately evident from Genesis 22 that one of the principal themes (and truly an overlooked theme, often overlooked in deference to the faith of Abraham), is that of the nature of God. I would like to emphasize the *nature* of God over and against the *role* of God in this text, as important as the role of God might be. To be sure, we have examined God's role and have an idea what this role is, but here the nature of God is central. As odd as it might appear, it is in this text, after a long and eventful journey since Genesis 12, that we are faced with one of the most challenging and difficult understandings of God. Perhaps it is because this kind of challenge resonates closely and personally with us that we are likely to wonder about such a divine command. We wonder silently, some of us for fear of retribution. At a most fundamental level, it seems that this passage raises questions about God—enough questions to hint at the possibility that the test could be more about God than Abraham.

For many of us, however, such a radical paradigm shift in thinking about this passage is enough to cause us to abandon such an idea. It seems to me that the questions and issues about God are such that neither do they leave us alone, nor can we, for that matter, leave them alone. They are questions about life and relationships and thus must be pursued. If anything, Genesis 22 compels us not to reduce God to manageable human categories that conform to our religious piety. Clearly this is not a God who allows us to move from Palm Sunday to Easter Sunday without the intervening darkness. Such a shortcut is unacceptable and, finally, impossible.

In Genesis 22:8, we have the principal statement of faith by Abraham that God will hold together the promise of Genesis 12 and the multiple demands of Genesis 22; God will provide. Of course such a statement of faith only makes sense if, indeed, what is to transpire lies beyond the human capacity to foresee. Abraham has had the experience of waiting and hoping, and finally of believing and knowing, that God will indeed provide.

As the literal journey of father and son begins, Abraham assures Isaac that God will provide (v. 8). This confessional statement combines both trust and vulnerability. Such an assuring statement is an altogether common feature in a parent/child relationship. From time to time, the child needs the parental assurance that all will be well; the child needs to believe that a parent has the power to assure that, indeed, all will be well. But here in this story, Abraham knows better; he knows that he cannot tell Isaac that all will be well through his parental resources. He knows that there is only one statement of assurance: "God will provide." It is ultimately God who must provide a way out of this test. Maybe more accurately, it is God who must fulfill this test. There is no circumventing the fact that the obligation to fulfill this test lies with God.

To the degree that the outcome of this test is out of Abraham's hands, he is vulnerable and dependent. Like so many instances throughout the Abraham narrative, here God's call is preeminent. It is God who provides the place of sacrifice, a place that Abraham will see in three days; for Abraham cannot see the place of sacrifice, and it will not be until the eleventh hour that he will see the "ram," again through God's initiative. God not only "sees"; but also an element of limitless vision characterizes God's provision. In this instance, "sight" reflects power. From Genesis 22:1 it is clear that God is the architect of these events, setting the stage for the entire horrific episode, and clearly it is God who envisions this final "test" and its fulfillment.

Abraham's response after the sacrifice of the ram is confessional. His confession in Genesis 22:14, "the Lord will provide," recalls his response to Isaac in Genesis 22:8. These two statements, as similar as they are, inform each other. When Abraham utters the words, "the Lord will provide," he invites us to understand the openness of the future that is being ascribed to God. God is bound by neither spatial nor temporal boundaries. Yes, this is about the ram, but this is about significantly more than the ram; it is about God's future.

But there is yet an additional issue at stake here. That Abraham expresses "the Lord will provide" demonstrates a quality of faith, and not a knowledge generated by human certainty. Subtle as it might be, this distinction is striking: Abraham has faith in God's future, but it is only God who knows the future; this is the faith expressed. In this story, only God knows—and Abraham *believes* that God knows. It seems to me that if Abraham had really known what could have transpired, if he had known, on the basis of his knowledge, that finally the sacrifice of his son would be unnecessary, then the story quickly would have relinquished its role as a "test," and would have become a farce. And if this farce had come to pass, then the harm done to Isaac would have been irreparable. It *must* be the case that Abraham does not know.

Like Abraham, we have faith, and we must hope in a future that often strikes us as bleak, without hope. To hope is what we must do. When we pray, "Lead us not into temptation," or as this is sometimes rendered, "do not put us to the test," we must believe in the genuine sense of the possibility of God's putting us to the test.

The seemingly irreconcilable tension between the *role* of God and the *nature* of God is worth exploring not only for itself but also particularly for the implications for the contemporary church. On the one hand, some Christians hold, either from personal experience or from some kind of other belief, that God "tests" humans, and that humans have little recourse for divine provision. In this scenario, the argument is that this is simply the ways things are, and since God is both omnipotent and inscrutable, God will "test" as God sees fit, and it is unlikely that we shall be able to discern why. Whereas on the surface this position would seem to have a particular kind of religious piety, at a deeper level it is problematic, as there is no corresponding role for a God who fulfills a promise, or who provides.

Moreover, the very well-established axiom that says, "God will not test us beyond our capacity to bear" (1 Cor 10:13) is a peculiar understanding of divine testing. Who can bear the death of a child (as one notable and ever-present scenario comes to mind readily)? Not surprising is that these positions are generated by a human understanding of how God functions in this world. This is not so much a criticism as an observation, understanding as humans that we do not have a choice but to think as humans. However, the challenge occurs when we seek to be exhaustive in our understanding and appropriation of God purely in terms of human categories. If it does nothing else, Genesis 22 serves as a reminder that finally we are ill equipped to comprehend fully the nature of God.

On the other hand, the theologically very important, though simple, refrain, "God will provide," cannot be employed as it often is, simply as a reflexive human response, again shrouded in the vocabulary of a particular religious piety. This position is problematic on at least two fronts. First, it has a platitudinous tone that overlooks and disregards circumstances and contexts. Second, divine provision is very difficult to challenge. Who indeed will challenge the idea that "God will provide"? It is an idea so deeply embedded in our religious psyches that to challenge hints at blasphemy. Some might even take the position and wonder to those who question whether they do not have the faith and trust that God will provide. But it seems to me that this kind of argument misses the point. This is certainly one response that seems to relieve humans of any responsibility. To utter "God will provide, God will provide," is analogous to Jeremiah's warning to the people of his day not to repeat ad nauseam, "The Temple of the Lord"; " The Temple of the Lord" as if somehow these words in and of themselves have salvific power (Jer 7:4). I would suggest that such a phrase (wrapped in the vocabulary of a particular piety void of context or action) is designed to be exclusionary since the implication is that some Christians have the knowledge that God will provide through the depth of their faith. Others who might dare to question or challenge the notion of God's provision might be viewed as lacking in sufficient faith. Whatever the argument, expression of piety is no excuse for inaction.

In this story enveloped by a narrative of sheer terror stand the indisputable bookends of God's role, reflecting central components of God's nature. Thus, in the midst of this tale that shocks us (and that surely must have done the same to Abraham and Sarah), is the very clear reminder that in the face of the prospects of abandonment and the further prospects of returning to barrenness, God acts. Even here, However, there is nothing universally uniform about such a position. We can ill afford this truth too to become an empty platitude. Those of us who read and study Genesis 22 are conditioned against the very tempting reality of trying to explain this story. At its very core, this story, like God, is unexplainable and perhaps incomprehensible; and, I believe, this story warns against simplistic reductions.

The fact is, the inscrutable nature of God is further accentuated here. As we witnessed in Genesis 21, it is in God's season and in God's time that God acts so that Sarah conceives and bears a son, and it is abundantly clear that in God's time, just as God gives, God might choose to take away. Nonetheless, we wonder: did God not promise?

Will this promise again be endangered—this time through a divine initiative? As we continue to ponder these questions, we finally arrive at a place where we can no longer employ the facilities of reason that we have become accustomed to using as a way of facing difficult issues or resolving problems. We must face the reality that human ingenuity and reasoning capacity are insufficient in seeking to understand how God functions.

As the story begins, "(And behold) after these things God tested Abraham" (v. 1), I find myself unable to move beyond these opening words. How could we contemplate fulfillment when the narrative of fulfillment begins in this manner? So "after these things," we are left to wonder, *what things*? Have Abraham and Sarah not been tested before, repeatedly? Up to this point, where this "test" now begins, we have had barrenness, deception, warfare, surrogacy, manipulation, destruction, incest, envy, jealousy, and rivalry, and now comes a "test." It is therefore not difficult to understand why this opening statement about God's testing Abraham would be shocking. It is right at the beginning point here that we are reminded that there is nothing routine about the hope of fulfillment. Testing might very well come even after the physical evidence of fulfillment—in this case, Isaac.

We do not know what the divine intent and hope are. From time to time in the biblical story, as readers, we are provided with information and insight that the subject of the story might not be aware of, but here there is no such information. Like Abraham, we too are left to wonder. "Take your son, your only son, your son whom you love" (v. 2). In these short, sharp, and pointed words lie a hint of the death of a hope, as if to suggest no mistaking about what is at stake (though for centuries there seems to have been some mistaking as to the statement, "your only son"). Perhaps as one would expect, there is no word from Abraham—an active response, yes, but silent. There is no discussion, no question, no argument, no "how could you ask this of me?" Nothing. Silence. And at least for a while, we are left to wonder about Abraham.

While I seek to be understanding toward Abraham, as difficult as it is, I find Abraham's lack of engagement with God at this point seriously problematic—unfairly so. But I find myself voiceless in the face of such silence. Certainly I am aware of my audacity in this regard, as

I place myself in a position of what appears to be that of judge. But I seek not to judge but to walk a line of wondering and concluding, questioning but not judging.

Was this not the same Abraham who a little while back challenged God on the basis of God's own established mercy and righteousness to spare Sodom and Gomorrah, cities of widespread evil? Fifty, forty-five, thirty, twenty, ten? But the challenge on behalf of Sodom and Gomorrah also tells us something about God: God listened; God acknowledged; God took Abraham and his voice seriously; God changed, and came to understand what can be construed as grace and mercy. So we have this very recent encounter, but now silence. How can we not wonder, when Abraham himself set the standard and model for engaging with and challenging God, by his having been the first to do so. And yet when God tells Abraham to offer Isaac as a burnt sacrifice, we are simply told: "And Abraham got up early in the morning" (Gen 22:1).

We further wonder if Abraham heard in God's command a sound, a tone, an irrefutable command that could not be negotiated with, spoken about, or challenged. As I think of this episode, I recall the encounter between Elijah and God as Elijah flees from Ahab and Jezebel (1 Kgs 19:1–18). Elijah trusts God enough to pour his heart out, to complain; he is ready to run far away from such evil, and then awaits the conventional modes of divine manifestations. But such manifestations are void. They are merely natural phenomena without divine presence. In the very sound of silence, God responds (1 Kgs 19:11–12). Silence has its place, but I wonder about Abraham. Genesis 22 says, "God will show him," literally translated, "God will say it to him" (v. 3). It is as if God knows and understands God as saying, "Trust me."

As if to underline the torturous nature of this journey, the words "father" and "son" are used twelve times separately; although some argue that the recurring words "father" and "son" are not necessarily pertinent for understanding this story, at the very least, the words "father" and "son" point to the poignancy of the story and certainly to the torturous nature of the journey. After Abraham and Isaac leave the "servants" behind (Gen 22:6, my translation), the journey becomes even more clearly one involving father and son—only—together, and seemingly worlds apart.

Not surprisingly the servants do not have a voice. They are told what to do, as was the custom for property. Thus even when they are present, they are voiceless: seen and not heard, as the saying goes. It seems to me that what makes this particular reference to "servants" relevant here is the fact that the same Hebrew word used for "servant" (*na'ar*) is used to describe Isaac. Thus, while we have the poignancy of "my son" and the numerous references to Isaac by name, we also have a reference to Isaac in an anonymous way with the word *na'ar*. This kind of distancing might very well reflect the importance of the event. Perhaps, just perhaps, if Abraham could bring himself to be distant, maybe, just maybe, some of the pain might dissipate. I doubt it, however. In this context, "My son" does not express any sense of anonymity or distancing. This kind of relational language, in the face of what is to come, is deeply poignant. I would further suggest that this is language of vulnerability; "my son" creates an inextricable connection between Abraham and Isaac, so much so that the sacrifice of Isaac is the sacrifice of Abraham.

When Abraham does indeed speak, we are still left to wonder, what does he mean when he says to the servants, "We will come back to you" (v. 5)? Is this again the faith of Abraham in the hope of a future that cannot be overcome? Maintaining an element of secrecy, Abraham proceeds with the "test." Abraham outlines a plan to the servants, indicating to them that they are on their way to worship, after which he and Isaac will return. On the one hand, one might be led to conclude that Abraham is so confident of the outcome of this test that he goes so far as to assure the servants that both father and son will return. One might further say that with his words to the servants, Abraham puts God to the test. Abraham does tell the truth to the servants: father and son will return. The trust in this regard is based on what Abraham has already experienced from God.

However apprised of the situation Isaac is, we do know that he is aware of a sacrifice to take place (v. 7). Even though the circumstances of Isaac and of the servants are different from each other, the reality is that both the servants and Isaac are essentially powerless. The rings of power are clearly delineated. God commands Abraham to sacrifice Isaac, but we are not told whether any information is given to Isaac. Is Abraham so aware of the impending horror that he himself is afraid?

If Abraham, because of his faith, is not afraid, then why does he not tell the truth to his servants or to Isaac? The text is simply silent. We have seen in this lengthy narrative even the role of deception at work. (We see such a theme elsewhere, as in 1 Samuel 16:2, where a deceptive plan is woven together to bring about that which God intends: the anointing of David as king.)

For us to gain the essence of the story in Genesis 22, I submit that it is not necessary for us to cast a positive blanket over such deception. As we have repeatedly witnessed in the narrative, God's ways are inscrutable, and God will employ whatever means necessary. Under the broad rubric of providing a land, descendants, and blessings, the promise bearer is about to be sacrificed.

The drama continues in an even more pronounced manner, and the parallels with the crucifixion event of Jesus are not lost on Christian readers: "Abraham took the wood of the burnt offering and laid it on his son Isaac and he himself carried the fire and knife. So the two of them walked on together" (v. 16). We simply cannot miss the power of this moment. Isaac, like Christ, carries the very element for his sacrifice. Just as Christian readers cannot separate the life of Christ from events surrounding his death, from here on, it will be impossible for readers to contemplate Isaac's role without taking into account the physical journey to the sacrifice.

Whatever else transpires, the sacrifice of Isaac is the turning point in the journey of the Abraham narratives. Isaac and Abraham carry all the elements. These two will physically bear the burden. As if to clarify further this moment between Abraham and Isaac, the servants who would ordinarily fetch the "heavy equipment" do not in any way participate in this specific aspect of the journey. Isaac suffers as a prelude to his sacrifice.

As to why Isaac might not have carried the knife and the fire, perhaps this is yet another moment when, at least for a little while, Abraham seeks to protect Isaac. But from whom? Or perhaps, as Trible suggests, "Isaac carries the wood that would ignite him. Yet unkindled it is not dangerous material, unlike the fire and the knife that Abraham takes in his own hand. The father embraced his son with potential destruction, even as he protects him from immediate danger."[2] Perhaps so. In any event, unlike Christ, Isaac does not fully know why he is carrying the sacrificial wood. Christ is made to carry the cross through the streets, and Isaac's sacrificial wood (like the cross) carries a representation and symbolism. Even the heavy burden of the sacrificial wood, which accentuates the drama, alludes to the weight that comes with being an object of sacrifice. Like Christ, Isaac in some respects calls out to his father; but at least for a while, there is both closeness and seeming incomprehensible distance. Perhaps under these circumstances the only fitting mode of being is that of silence—really what is there to say!

Elie Wiesel, who himself lived through (more accurately, survived) the Holocaust, suggests, "one went to face death, the other to give it, but they went together, still close to one another, though everything separated them."[3] In Wiesel's *Night*, he relates the poignant experience of finding his father in the confines of the concentration camp after he thought they had been separated forever: "He was standing near the wall, bowed down, his shoulders sagging as though beneath a heavy burden. I went to him, took his hand and kissed it. A tear fell upon it. Whose was that tear? Mine? His? I said nothing, nor did he. We had never understood one another so clearly."[4] Wiesel and his father, in the context of the Holocaust, were silent as they held each other. It is the essence of closeness and the bonding of the spirit. In the face of Isaac's holocaust, there is also silence and togetherness in the midst of the distance. Perhaps there are moments when silence is the sole sound, as nothing of the magnitude of Isaac's sacrifice or Jesus's crucifixion can be understood with words. Again we discover that hope of fulfillment can never be fulfilled in the ordinary.

How can we begin to understand the silence and the nonresistance of Isaac (Gen 22:9)? I do find this inexplicable, but then again, it seems truly beyond our reach. To say that Isaac's submission is beyond our reach is not in any way to imply that we should not ask questions about it. This is yet another aspect of our challenge: we ask questions knowing that even as we do so, answers are not always or easily forthcoming. Is Isaac's silence a sense of resignation to the in-

---

2. Trible, "Genesis 22: The Sacrifice of Sarah," 175.

3. Wiesel, "Sacrifice of Isaac," 81.

4. Wiesel, *Night,* 79.

evitable death, or, in fact, is there a deeper understanding of his role? Regardless, we are left to wonder what went though the very heart of Isaac. Must there not have been some internal conflict between trust and unquestioning obedience? We are left to wonder what this experience will do to the faith and trust of Isaac.

Perhaps in movies eleventh-hour rescues are sensational, and they certainly heighten the dramatic effect. Indeed, in far too many instances, this kind of cinematic spectacle has become the norm. But, of course, Genesis 22 is not such a spectacle, and I believe that this story builds faith and trust. If indeed this story does build faith and trust, then is the intent here to cause Abraham to trust or to be indebted? I suggest that the language of indebtedness is the language of enslavement.

Indeed, as the narrative reaches it dramatic denouement, several elements remind us of the direction, subject, and power of fulfillment in the story. There is a hint of conditionality to the promise as the narrative in Genesis 22 ends. As we would expect, throughout the journey, God places certain expectations on Abraham and Sarah, but never quite a condition. Perhaps then this was a test of a significantly higher order than what Abraham and Sarah had previously experienced or imagined. We are told that it is *because* of Abraham's willingness to release Isaac that Yahweh *will indeed bless* him. Prior to this, the narrative never hinted at the promise being conditional and there is certainly no further discussion in the narrative of such a significant component as a divine condition.

As Genesis 22 ends, the singular voice of God dominates the scene, and this in turn leaves no doubt as to the one with absolute power; the one who makes the promise is the one who provides, and we are not surprised that both Abraham and Isaac are voiceless at the end. To underline further the reality that fulfillment is in the realm of the divine, some questions are answered at the end; other questions remain unanswered, and it seems that the narrative does not seek to elucidate readers about possibilities. Is there estrangement between father and son? Given that the text does not provide certainties for us, we may draw conclusions from inferences only to a limited extent. But this is more than a matter of curiosity.

We are reminded that even after there is fulfillment and hope for the future, questions and challenges still remain. Always there will be questions; with hope comes many aspects of new and renewed life, but hope and fulfillment do not exhaust life's challenges. To point to a much larger issue within the Bible, the reality is that the inscrutable God works in mysterious ways, and despite the best human efforts, some things will always remain a mystery—perhaps *must* always a remain a mystery.

ABRAHAM AND JOB: RIGHTEOUSNESS TO THE TEST

Whereas the stories of Abraham and Job are very different in both substance and circumstances, it seems that as we reflect on the hope of fulfillment, aspects of Job not only parallel those of Abraham in this narrative, but also the story of Job further informs the manner in which we might read and appropriate the "test" in Genesis 22.

We are made aware, abundantly so, that the righteous person (be it Abraham or Job, arguably the two most notable examples in the Old Testament) is not exempt from divine testing. While some Christians believe that such testing, for Christians, indicates a certain level of faith attained and might be viewed as a badge of honor, this position finally collapses. The reality is that the faithful and the righteous are tested, but this does not necessarily mean that in an odd way these "righteous ones" should be elevated to a higher status in the eyes of the community. Moreover, it seems to me that we must be careful here as not to make universal claims about the particularities of God's testing. The fact is, we do know that not all, indeed few, instances of divine testing result in the manner of Abraham's and Job's experiences. Of course even here, as we have witnessed, both stories end with a note of questioning and not with a little uncertainty. We may safely suggest that, finally, the direction of the story and its ending are as much for readers who struggle with these themes as it is for textual resolution.

Certainly like all Christians, the "righteous" (whoever determines such a designation) are put to the test, and none of us should expect otherwise, and none of us should expect a privileged status in this regard. One of the clearest ideas expressed in the Prologue of Job is the recurring theme of Job's righteousness. Not only does the community acknowledge the righteousness of Job, but also more significant, God thus acknowledges him. Thus even before the "test" of Job, we know that God sees Job as righteous. This is significant in that it makes clear that one's righteousness (even at the exalted level of Abraham and Job) finally will not exempt one from divine testing.

Moreover, we know that like Job, Abraham is faithful—fractured but faithful. We know this; God knows this; but the "test" proceeds nonetheless. When "the dust settles," both Abraham and Job will come to know God in different ways, but not yet perfectly. Both Abraham and Job, having been deemed faithful and righteous, are "tested" beyond anything they could have imagined; in observing their encounters with God, we are reminded that we learn a great deal about God in a way that is beyond human capacity. We therefore cannot imagine that human comprehension captures the fullness of God's capacity and the radicality of God's actions. Like Abraham and Job, we must live the tension of hope knowing that the God in whom we believe both gives and takes away. Abraham knows this, and Job responds to his ordeal with an even more precise statement of this truth (Job 1:21).

BIBLIOGRAPHY

Brueggemann, Walter. *Genesis*. Interpretation. Atlanta: John Knox, 1982.

Fretheim, Terence E. "Genesis." In *New Interpreter's Bible,* edited by Leander E. Keck, 1:319–674. Nashville: Abingdon, 1994.

———. "Jacob in Tradition." *Interpretation* 26 (1972) 419–36.

Frymer-Kensky, Tikva. "Hagar in the Hebrew Bible." In *Women in Scripture,* edited by Carol Meyers, 86–87. Grand Rapids: Eerdmans, 2000.

———. "Patriarchal Family Relationships and Near Eastern Law." *Biblical Archaeologist* 44 (1981) 209–14.

———. "Sarai/Sarah in the Hebrew Bible." In *Women in Scripture,* edited by Carol Meyers, 150–51. Grand Rapids: Eerdmans, 2000.

Gossai, Hemchand. *Power and Marginality in the Abraham Narrative.* Lanham, MD: University Press of America, 1995.

Gunkel, Hermann. "The Jacob Traditions." In *Water for a Thirsty Land: Israelite Literature and Religion,* edited by K. C. Hanson, 42–67. Fortress Classics in Biblical Studies. Minneapolis: Fortress, 2001.

———. "The Hagar Traditions." In *Water for a Thirsty Land: Israelite Literature and Religion,* edited by K. C. Hanson, 68–84. Fortress Classics in Biblical Studies. Minneapolis: Fortress, 2001.

Millard, A. R. "Abraham." In *Anchor Bible Dictionary,* edited by David Noel Freedman, 35–41. New York: Doubleday, 1991.

Rad, Gerhard von. *Genesis.* Translated by John H. Marks. Rev. ed. Old Testament Library. Philadelphia: Westminster, 1972.

Sarna, Nahum M. *Genesis.* JPS Torah Commentary. Philadelphia: Jewish Publication Society, 1989.

———. *Understanding Genesis.* New York: Jewish Theological Seminary of America, 1966.

Terrien, Samuel L. *Till The Heart Sings: A Biblical Theology of Manhood and Womanhood.* 1985. Reprinted, Grand Rapids: Eerdmans, 2004.

Thompson, Thomas L. "Conflict Themes in the Jacob Traditions." *Semeia* 15 (1979) 5–26.

Trible, Phyllis. "Genesis 22: The Sacrifice of Sarah." In *"Not in Heaven": Coherence and Complexity in Biblical Narrative,* edited by Jason Rosenblatt and Joseph Sitterson, 170–91. Indiana University Press, 1991; reprinted in *Women in the Hebrew Bible: A Reader,* edited by Alice Bach, 271–90. New York: Routledge, 1999.

———. "Hagar: The Desolation of Rejection." In *Texts of Terror: Literary-Feminist Readings of Biblical Tradition,* 9–35. Overtures to Biblical Theology. Philadelphia: Fortress, 1984.

———. *Texts of Terror: Literary-Feminist Readings of Biblical Tradition.* Overtures to Biblical Theology. Philadelphia: Fortress, 1984.

Westermann, Claus. *Genesis 12–36.* Translated by John J. Scullion. Continental Commentaries. Minneapolis: Augsburg, 1985.

Wiesel, Elie. *Night.* Translated by Stella Rodway. New York: Farrar, Straus & Giroux, 1960.